Message
OF THE
Cameos

Message OF THE Cameos

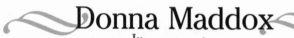 **Donna Maddox**

Illustrations by
Stephen S. Sawyer

Aldersgate Resources
Franklin, Tennessee

Printed in the United States of America

05   04   03   02   01   1   2   3   4   5

Library of Congress Catalog Card Number: 2001091670

ISBN: 1-57736-241-1

Cover design by Gary Bozeman

All Scripture quotations, unless otherwise indicated, are taken from the HOLY BIBLE, NEW INTERNATIONAL VERSION®. NIV®. Copyright © 1973, 1978, 1984 by International Bible Society. Used by permission of Zondervan Publishing House. All rights reserved.

Scripture quotations marked (NKJV) are taken from the New King James Version. Copyright © 1982 by Thomas Nelson, Inc. Used by permission. All rights reserved.

Scripture quotations marked (PHILLIPS) are taken from *The New Testament in Modern English*, translated by J.B. Phillips. Copyright © 1960 by Macmillan Company. Used by permission. All rights reserved.

Cameos and illustrations by Stephen S. Sawyer
143 Lexington St.
Versailles, Ky 40383
www.ART4GOD.com
1-888-ART4GOD

Aldersgate Resources
PROVIDENCE HOUSE PUBLISHERS
Aldersgate Renewal Ministries
United Methodist Renewal Services Fellowship
121 East Avenue Goodlettsville, Tennessee 37072
615-851-9192

Providence Publishing Corporation
238 Seaboard Lane Franklin, Tennessee 37067
800-321-5692
www.providencehouse.com

To Jesus, the Christ, the Son of the living God.

He is the rock on which we can build our lives. As a house
stands firm when built on rock, so does the human life
remain secure, even in troubled times, when that life is
built on the Rock, Jesus.

In writing this book, I have prayed that my thoughts
would be His thoughts and that He would bring to my
mind those things that He would have me share.
The figure raised in relief in each of these "gems" in my
life is that of Jesus who, through the Holy Spirit,
teaches me and fills my life with God's love.

Contents

Foreword

The Message of the Cameos is an intriguing approach to recording a personal testimony of what it means to live in the Holy Spirit, the Spirit of Jesus Christ.

Donna Maddox presents a compelling, winsome, and believable witness to the reality of "Christ in me" through glimpses into her everyday life. What others might see as mere coincidences, Donna views as Providence, the guiding hand of God, being led by the Spirit, or the presence of the Lord. For her, life is simple: "Trust in the Lord with all your heart and lean not on your own understanding; in all your ways acknowledge him, and he will make your paths straight" (Proverbs 3:5–6 NIV).

I've known Donna for many years. Like the Velveteen Rabbit, she is "real." She has a simple trust in God, and she attempts to live her life with integrity and consistency in both religious and secular circles. Her testimony is not filled with the drama of deliverance from a decadent lifestyle. Rather, it is the story of a woman who had the opportunity to meet Jesus at an early age and has enjoyed the advantage of having Him as her friend and teacher ever since. She has lived her life praising God for His goodness, giving thanks for God's blessings, and trusting God in times of struggle and pain. It is a testimony that I pray for my grandchildren to experience.

Donna sees each experience of her life as being carefully and skillfully carved like a cameo with the figure of Jesus raised in relief. When you look at her life, Jesus is what she desires for you to see. For me, that's the great adventure of the Christian life. The writer of Hebrews tells us that Jesus is the "exact image" of God (Hebrews 1:3). When you look at Jesus, you see God. In 2 Corinthians 3:18, Paul talks about us "being transformed into his likeness with ever-increasing glory." When others look at a Christian, they should see Jesus lifted up. As we live in Christ and Christ lives in us, we should experience a transformation, by the power of the Holy Spirit, that changes us to look like, feel like, talk like, act like, and love like Jesus. I believe that Donna has successfully communicated this truth in her book.

Every reader should be blessed, and encouraged, that it is possible to be a real Christian.

Gary Moore
Executive Director, Aldersgate Renewal Ministries
An affiliate of the General Board of Discipleship of the
United Methodist Church through the Upper Room

Preface

You are not holding this book by chance. If you are reading these words it is because God is reaching out to you, and there is something in this book that He wants you to know.

One of the most amazing things about writing this book is that the Lord awakened me between 5:00 and 6:00 A.M. each morning to write. Even though I am not a morning person, I eagerly climbed out of bed the minute I awoke! I was excited knowing He was there with me and would soon show me something to share. I could actually feel His presence with me each morning as He taught me what to write.

Just as a carved cameo lifts a recognizable figure in relief from a gem, each chapter in this book is a cameo from my life that clearly lifts Jesus and the Holy Spirit in a recognizable way.

For years I have labored over everything I needed to write whether it was a letter, a term paper, a press release, a course I was teaching, or a talk I was delivering. It took days before I completed the task, going back and adding something, changing something, or starting over with a new focus. Not so with this book! Each cameo flowed as I typed on the computer. Each cameo, with few exceptions, was completed in a single morning.

Each morning I would sit at my computer and pray for the Lord to bring to my mind anything that was important that He wanted me to share. Sometimes I knew immediately what to write. Other mornings I would sit in prayer longer with the bright screen of my computer in front of me as I waited. The thoughts and words always came, and I cherished this time with Him.

Some mornings I would begin writing about one thing, but before I knew it, I was writing about something different or, in some cases, something long forgotten. Often He gave me important insights into His word . . . like His word is a way of life. No matter which century we live in, how long or short our hair is, or how much education or money we have, or don't have, we all have the same basic needs. We all struggle with overcoming our human nature—such things as anger, bitterness, resentment, and hate—and we strive to produce the fruit of the Spirit: love, joy, peace, patience, kindness, goodness, faithfulness, gentleness, and self control (Gal. 5:19–23).

Writing this book has done for me what I believe reading it will do for you. In writing it, I have found God at work in my life in ways I had not recognized before. I believe that as you read this book, He will reach out to you and that you will recognize Him in your own life in many new ways or, perhaps, for the first time.

Acknowledgments

With love and gratitude I thank the following: My mother and grandmother (Granny) who taught me from birth that Jesus loves me and is my friend.

Aunt Martha (Auntie) and Uncle Bob (Unkie) McConnell.

My wonderful family where God placed me to be loved, nurtured, disciplined, and encouraged to grow in Him.

Family and friends who both loved me and caused me to suffer when I was a child, for in each situation I have learned and grown stronger through prayer.

My son, who has brought laughter, love, and joy into my life and continues to amaze me with his strength and courage.

Bob, my wonderful husband, who has loved me and encouraged me over the years. He has patiently and lovingly assisted me in every possible way in the writing and publication of this book.

My lifelong friends Poppy, Marcelene, and Nancy, who last year encouraged me with much excitement to complete this book, which at that time consisted of only three cameos.

Jo, who took hours out of her time on the beach to proofread a rough draft of my manuscript. She also encouraged me to publish this book.

Ellie, my dear friend and advisor.

Stephen Sawyer, who not only carved the cameos for the cover and the last page of the book, but also created most of the illustrations. His wife, Cindy, has been a great supporter too.

Vanderbilt University School of Nursing, for my professional and continuing education, which has in recent years included computer support that ultimately enabled me to write this book.

Radford University, for providing me with an excellent education from kindergarten through sixth grade, at their elementary school, and later college. I am grateful for their outstanding professors, especially Dr. Minor Wine Thomas.

Aldersgate Renewal Ministries, whose staff read the manuscript, assisted with the selection of appropriate Scriptures, and graciously offered to endorse this book as part of their Aldersgate Resources imprint.

Message of the Cameos

The whole adventure did not begin with the dream, but this book is the result of the dream. "You will be a cameo writer," I was told in a dream. "You will write like the books of Ruth and Esther."

When I awoke, the dream was very real to me. In my mind, I could still see the pale green and white cameos of my dream with three people nearby. "Wonder if this means anything?" I asked myself. I wrote about the dream in my notebook, which was a sort of journal that I sometimes kept, but not always.

Is there such a thing as a written cameo? I had certainly never heard of one. I only knew about the carved cameo jewelry. On my way to the den to look up the word cameo in our large Webster's Dictionary, I felt I should instead go to my office and look it up in the dictionary in my desk drawer. Obediently, I went to my office and retrieved the *Webster's New World Dictionary,* Revised Popular Library Pocket-Sized Edition Copyright 1977. My heart nearly exploded as I read the words describing "cameo."

cam-e-o (kam'eo', kam'yo) n., pl. -os 1. A gem carved with a figure raised in relief. 2. a) an outstanding bit role. b) A bit of fine writing.

Having a curious nature, I later checked the definition in the big dictionary in the den. It added to what I had just read. It stated "b" above as a "brief literary or filmic piece that brings into delicate or sharp relief the character of a person, place or event."

I have always wanted to write a book and have felt that God wanted me to write about some of the things that He has taught me. I have, however, always been overwhelmed at the thought of writing a book. Now that I understood that a cameo was a short story with a single theme, I was excited, because I had already written several cameos without realizing what they were. I had written each of them to demonstrate a single theme showing God's help in a specific way. One cameo related a situation showing His love, another His power, and another detailed His guidance through a desperate situation. I had used the cameos to teach specific topics during Life in the Spirit Seminars (LISS) which are offered to church congregations by Aldersgate Renewal Ministries (ARM) whose mission is "bringing the life of the Holy Spirit into the life of the church."

Four or five years passed after I had the cameo dream. I had almost forgotten about it when, one day, as I was preparing a talk on the spirit of prayer for a LISS weekend, I came across a folder containing some of my notes of dreams. On top was the description of my dream about being a cameo writer. I had all but forgotten about it! From that day forward the Holy Spirit constantly reminded me that I was to write. I simply could not get it off my mind.

Just before I left for the LISS weekend, I had a manicure. The lady that does my nails said, "I have a new polish I want you to try. It is really pretty and I know you will like it. It is called 'Cameo.'" Well, I wore Cameo nail polish on the LISS weekend, and each time I looked at my hands I saw cameo polish.

As we were gathering in the parking lot on Sunday (I had given my talk on the Spirit of Prayer on Saturday) one of our leaders said, "Donna, you write out your talks so perfectly.

A couple of us wondered if you have ever thought about writing a book." I believed that this was definitely confirmation for me to write a book! I was beginning to get excited about it as "cameo" was coming at me from just about everywhere. At home that night Bob and I watched an old movie on television. Later, in bed, we were talking about Audrey Hepburn when Bob mentioned the fact that she had a cameo role in the movie *Always*.

On Monday, after the LISS weekend, I went to a dress shop to pick up a blouse that was being held for me. The lady behind the counter had a lovely, rather large, gold cross on a chain around her neck. I commented on its beauty, and as she reached up to touch the cross I noticed that she had on her finger a very beautiful cameo ring! The ring was so unusual! It was a brown stone with a white head raised in relief.

There was no doubt in my mind that, with God's help, I would become a cameo writer.

Introduction

Granny held my hand as I skipped along beside her on our adventure down Washington Street in Petersburg, Virginia. It was a warm, sunny day, and I was excited because Granny was visiting us, and she loved me very much. I knew she loved me, because she read to me at night, played "This Little Piggy" with my toes, and rocked me in her lap. She often cut an apple in half and took a spoon and scraped the apple into the spoon and fed it to me "like I was a little bird." Sometimes she put me on her knee and let me pretend that I was on a horse. Bouncing me up and down on her knee, she showed me how the "ladies ride . . . and then the gentlemen ride . . . and finally, with a gallop, how the countrymen ride."

Because I was only three years old, it is amazing how well I remember our walk that warm summer afternoon. We had gone only a short distance from my parents' apartment when we came to a Catholic church. Granny, still holding my hand, led me up the steps to the church, pushed open the very large brown door, and we stepped inside. It was cool and rather dark, but more beautiful than anything I had ever seen. All around the room candles flickered through red glass containers in the dim light.

As I looked down the aisle at the front of the church I saw, leaning against a wall, a very large cross with a man nailed to it. My voice seemed to echo through the church as I whispered to Granny, "Who is that man?" Although I don't remember how she explained to me who Jesus is, I do remember that after answering my question, she asked me if I wanted to go up and kiss his feet. I didn't think I wanted to do that, but she held my hand firmly and began walking down the aisle toward the front of the church. I was pretty scared and sort of hanging on to her skirt hoping to pull her back. Granny walked, pretty much dragging me along, right up to the foot of the cross.

She knelt in front of the cross and kissed His feet. I knelt like she did and kissed His feet too. My fear left me, and, at that moment, Jesus became very real to me. From that moment on He became my friend in good times and my helper in difficult times. Often, over the next few years, I returned to pray alone in that beautiful and special church, each time having to look up to see Jesus. The cross, for some special reason, had been lowered on my first visit when Granny and I were there. On all of my other visits, Jesus' cross was raised high above the altar.

I was fortunate to meet Jesus at such an early age because it gave me an opportunity to truly accept Him as a child. Through the years I became quite disciplined in trying to live according to the Scriptures. When faced with difficult decisions, I often asked myself "What would Jesus do?" No matter how difficult it was to do what I thought He would do, that was the choice I made. As I grew into my teen years, I continued to pray, but lost some of the disciplined life I had experienced in those early years.

While I was no more "saved" than the person who accepts Jesus as their Lord and Savior on their deathbed, I had the advantage of having Him as my friend and teacher all of my life. What an awesome blessing this has been for me! This book is filled with cameos showing how the Holy Spirit taught, guided, and directed me as a child, adolescent, young adult, and now as a grandmother enjoying life and still learning through the autumn years.

We kissed the feet of Jesus.

Since this book skips quickly through the years, it is only here that I can introduce you to the parents and family where God placed me. Most of my life was difficult, but remember, I had the Holy Spirit guiding and leading me through it.

Mother was a petite, beautiful brunette who had worked hard all of her life. She was the third youngest of thirteen children. When she was in the fifth grade, both her mother and father became terminally ill, and Mother had to quit school and go to work to help support them and her younger brother and sister. She worked as a waitress in a downtown restaurant for a family that had owned the restaurant for many years. Miss Hattie was the manager, and she taught Mother that "anything worth doing is worth doing well," something that Mother always stressed to me. Miss Hattie became Mother's friend and mentor. Miss Hattie was killed in a car accident when I was only six, and I remember seeing her dressed in a peach-colored robe laying in a casket. I remember Mother crying. Miss Hattie was the first person I knew who died, and Mother had to explain death to me.

When she was in her late twenties, Mother met and married my daddy whom she thought was the "cutest little thing" and "the finest person" she had ever known. She had fallen in love not only with him, but also with his mother (Granny), and his two sisters, my Aunt Ruth and Aunt Martha.

Among my cherished memories are Mother and I kneeling together to say prayers. Mother often lovingly laughed at how one night when I was little and she and I were praying that I asked her to tell Him about Aunt Nettie's side. "Tell Him just how it hurts!" I told her. All of my life I have talked with Him and shared with Him my innermost fears and dreams.

In most of my childhood memories, Mother and Daddy were separated. They divorced when I was eight. Mother had to continue working, and since she had no one she could trust to keep me at home, I went to live with Aunt Martha and Uncle Bob (Auntie and Unkie) who lived in Radford, about six hours away. I was in kindergarten when I first went to live with them. Through the years, I traveled by train, in the conductor's care, to and from Radford and Petersburg. The one loving, stable figure in my life was Granny, whom I loved with all my heart. Granny died when I was eleven and after almost collapsing with grief, I forgot much about her. Only now, nearly fifty years later, am I beginning to recall the many wonderful times we shared, the gifts she gave me, and the love we had for each other.

Unkie was a dentist, and his father, Dr. John Preston McConnell, was the founder and the first president of Radford State Teachers' College, now Radford University. Because Mother had little formal education and had no opportunity to attend symphonies and other cultural events, I learned a whole new set of social standards and proper English from living with my aunt and uncle. I soon learned to "shift gears" from one lifestyle to the other without even thinking about it. Most of this shifting or transitioning, I believe, must have taken place while I was traveling on the train between cities and between the two separate lives that I lived.

A major thing I learned through this opportunity to live in two different settings was that people are the same in all walks of life. Only their lifestyles are different. They all have desires, dreams, difficulties, and fears. They all search for love and acceptance. In other words, we all have the same battles raging and the same things to overcome. Jesus' words are for everyone, in all walks of life, throughout all time. What He has given is for all.

Summers were spent with Mother in Petersburg and in the country with Granny at Plantersville. I spent most holidays with Mother, but during the school year, I lived in Radford with Auntie and Unkie.

Visiting Granny meant long, wonderful days ending with bedtime prayers together each night in the living room with Aunt Ruth and Uncle Macon, who also lived at Granny's. There were ice cream suppers, Children's Day programs, church revivals, and Sundays at the little church that the

Holy Spirit, working through Granny, had founded more than thirty years before.

Granny always wanted me to be a nurse, so after graduation from high school, with little thought of another career, I attended Vanderbilt University School of Nursing. My first two years there were filled with too many dates and too many good times. My grades suffered, and when my boyfriend flunked out and I made a D in a clinical nursing course, it was necessary for me to reevaluate my life. I transferred to Radford University, where I majored in psychology and lived at home with Auntie and Unkie. One course and one professor there (as told in the cameo "Image of God") changed my life.

After receiving a bachelor's degree with honors from Radford University, I worked for a year, first in the display department and later in sales at Neiman Marcus in Dallas, Texas. Through the leading of the Holy Spirit, I left Dallas and two exciting career offers in Texas to return to Petersburg, where I found Mother very ill and in need of my help. During the time I was with her, Mother had surgery and recuperated at home. To help support Mother and me, I taught fifth grade, allowing the teacher to leave his contract early.

The following summer I returned to Radford where I had been offered a summer position as a psychometrist at a mental health center. That fall I returned to Vanderbilt where I later graduated with a bachelor's degree with a major in nursing. The same summer I married a senior law student. The following year he and I moved to his hometown in Tennessee.

My husband did not plan a political career, but in 1965, the year our son was born, he ran for a political office and won by a landslide. It was easy for me to help him with his campaign because I had mingled with people from all walks of life since childhood. I felt at home with everyone. I enjoyed the political rallies, cakewalks, and long hours at the polls. I loved being his wife, and I loved being a mother.

Almost all of my life I have felt that God has had me "in training" for something special. This book is about that training. Each cameo relates significant works and teachings of the Holy Spirit to everyday life, beginning in childhood and continuing throughout the years of my life. This book is simply one person's love story!

～

"And we know that in all things God works for the good of those who love him, who have been called according to his purpose."
—Romans 8:28 NIV—

Message
OF THE
Cameos

Image on the Cameo

As I completed the early morning writing of one of the first cameos, I had a strong urge to send it to a Spirit-filled pastor and friend. I e-mailed it to her and asked her opinion on its content and possible use in ministry. When I saw her the next day, she told me that she was touched by my words and would like to talk with me soon. A couple of days later I sat in her office and explained the dream in which I was told that I would be a cameo writer. I mentioned the definitions of "cameo" which I had read. She was supportive of my writing and encouraged me to continue.

My excitement mounted when I saw her again several days later, and she told me that she had a *word* for me. I was to search the history of cameos where I would find *something important for my book*.

After searching the Internet for history of cameos and finding nothing helpful, I e-mailed a note to my half-sister (we share the same father), a librarian, and asked if she had suggestions of where to find the history of cameos.

The next morning I arose early, sat in front of my computer, and began my morning prayer, asking the Lord to give me recollection of the cameo to write that day. After prayer, I decided to check my e-mail before beginning to write. There was mail from my sister! She had sent a wonderful article on cameos. Along with the article, she had also suggested a web site where I could check for further information.

Immediately I read "The Mythological Messages of Cameos," by Anna M. Miller (*Jewelers' Circular Keystone,*

June 1999, v. 170 no. 6, pp. 232–33). An abstract written about the article says the best cameos are depictions of the Roman god of love, Cupid, and he is often used to convey such messages as "a secret love" and "love conquers all." According to Ms. Miller, "There's more to a cameo than the image of an anonymous woman carved in shell. . . . The cameos with the greatest appeal are those with a message, usually one of love."

My heart almost stood still. God is love! The Bible tells us in 1 John 4:16 that ". . . *God is love and he who abides in love abides in God, and God in him.*" Each cameo that I write shows God's love in my life. Each one lifts Jesus up as my Savior, friend, lover, and the center of my life. He, through the Holy Spirit, is my teacher and guide. His love shines forth in each cameo. A cameo gem with Jesus, the Holy Spirit, and the love of God somehow raised in relief on a shell or precious stone would be a beautiful and wonderful treasure. Only He would be able to inspire such a beautiful concept.

Over breakfast I shared with my husband the article my sister had sent. He made some interesting comments. He mentioned one thing that helps me see how all of the parts fit together perfectly for my cameo writing. "The root word 'cam'," he said, "means room or box. Single, particular, or specific rooms, like a den, an office, a sunroom, etc., are single-theme rooms. Those Easter eggs that have a creation inside that you can see when you peep through the hole in it, is a room, or 'cam.'"

As I was writing this cameo, I was led to retrieve an article that I read (by chance?) in the newspaper the day before. The Lord showed me that He wanted it to be included here. The article, titled "'New' prayer technique goes deep. Monk demonstrating ancient method in the Midstate," appeared in the Saturday, February 5, 2000, *Tennessean*. Ray Waddle, religion editor, wrote that for Father Thomas Keating, "the search for God starts by entering a room, the private inner room of the soul. There, a person finds God waiting, beyond the noise, beeps and defeats of life 'outside.'"

According to Keating, a Catholic monk and author based in a Colorado monastery, "Our purpose is to visit that place where the Father is waiting for us, and when we take on the discipline of relating to God in the 'private room', something like psychological healing of the most profound kind happens. Our goodness is affirmed."

Father Thomas Keating teaches "centering prayer," a twenty-minute spiritual exercise, which is a form of silent prayer for pondering passages from the Bible and emptying the mind of other thoughts to allow a fresh encounter with the divine and allow greater spiritual depth. "Prayer is relationship with God," Keating said in an interview, "and like any friendship, it grows."

Keating suggests that Jesus may have taught a version of centering prayer to His disciples. The evidence is Matthew 6:6, *"But whenever you pray go into your room and shut the door and pray to your Father who is in secret; and your Father who sees in secret will reward you."* "I think the 'room' is obviously a metaphor," Keating said. "They didn't have private rooms. They were lucky to have a room at all. The private room is the spiritual level of our being."

Wow!

CAMEO 2

I love u

𝒜s mentioned earlier, the Lord awakens me early, and I have been getting up to enjoy time with Him and write as He leads me. This morning I awoke and decided to go back to sleep. I

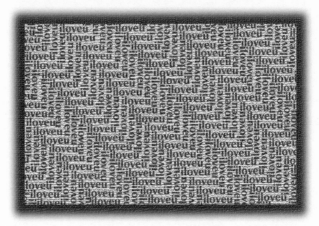

I carefully studied the mat . . .

started dreaming. There was a rug or mat under my feet with an interesting pattern on it. I started looking more carefully at it and discovered the pattern was "iloveu." This is the password I use for opening my computer. Immediately, I awoke knowing that the Lord had given me a dream connected with my computer. It was surely to remind me to get up and write. I couldn't help but smile and say, "iloveu2Lord."

CAMEO 3

Mother's Vision

As a child, I spent several weeks during most summers with my grandmother at her home in Plantersville, Virginia.

Plantersville was the community where my grandfather had opened his country store in the late 1800s. The original store, located about seventeen miles from Chase City where my grandfather lived and had another store, was a large room with a small bedroom behind it. When he married my grandmother in 1897, he added a kitchen, living room, front and back porches, and three bedrooms over the store-house. The old "store room" of the house had been closed years ago, after his death, and now only once in a while did anyone go in there. The room was full of memorabilia from the days when it was a country store. There was a large counter, scales, and an iron beehive that housed string. The beehive had a hole in the top for the string to be pulled through. There was lots of "stuff" covered with dust and surrounded by memories for my widowed grandmother and her daughter, Ruth. Aunt Ruth and her husband, Macon, lived with my grandmother. One particular summer the Holy Spirit worked in a special way through my mother—I suspect to save my life.

I had a grand time playing with children who lived down the road from us. There were several children in the family, and three of the youngest were about my age. Two were twins. It was their duty to "watch the cow" during the day and see that she had plenty of food and did not wander off or get hurt. I would often join them so we could play while we "watched" the cow.

I remember one particular day that we "watched the cow." I took a set of doll dishes and joined my playmates in the nearby field on the edge of the woods where the cow was grazing that day. They were happy to see me. Since I had the dishes with me, one of the playmates, the boy in the group, thought it would be fun to play "soda fountain." We tied the cow under a peach tree where she had plenty of grass to eat. We made a countertop out of an old plank we found nearby and supported it by using small logs as legs. We took a pitcher or jar they had, and three of us left to get water from a spring that was about a quarter of a mile into the woods while the fourth stayed with the cow.

We pretended that we were running a soda fountain. We took turns working behind the counter while the others visited the soda shop and ordered something to eat and/or drink. Our menu consisted of green peaches from the tree, warm milk, which was obtained by using the spigots (udders) of the cow, and cold water that we brought up the hill from the spring. We used my doll dishes to serve what was ordered. It was especially fun for me to serve behind the counter because I learned a new skill: how to milk the cow! Although it looked quite easy when the others did it, I had to learn the "gentle grasp and squeeze" necessary to obtain milk when someone ordered it. It was also fun to pick a peach from the tree, or pour a glass of water. We all enjoyed taking turns being the customer and working behind the counter.

During that summer at Granny's, I developed some little sores on my face around my nose. They kept getting worse, and soon got inside my nostrils. Aunt Ruth and Granny didn't think much about the sores since I usually had chigger bites and mosquito bites from playing in the woods and fields.

We had no electricity, telephones, or indoor plumbing that far out into the country where we lived. Light was obtained from oil lamps, and wood or coal was burned in the winter for heat. We had a very nice outhouse located only a short walk into the woods from the back of the house. My Uncle Macon was the superintendent of schools in Lunenburg County where we lived. His office was in Victoria, Virginia, about twenty miles away.

My mother lived in Petersburg, which was a four- or five-hour drive away from Plantersville. She and Daddy had been separated for several years, and Mother lived alone. Because she lived in an apartment building a short distance from a grocery store and just three blocks from downtown where she worked, she did not need a car. One morning, just as she awakened she said she saw me coming toward her with sores on my face. She was so concerned about me after this "vision" that she got off from work that day, rode a bus to Victoria, and went to Uncle Macon's office so she could ride home with him that afternoon.

When she got out of the car with him that afternoon we were all surprised to see her, and I was especially thrilled! I loved Mother with all my heart and wished that I could live with her. Granny loved seeing her to. Imagine how my mother felt when I ran to greet her and had sores on my face. "You need to go to the doctor," she said immediately. Aunt Ruth and Granny thought that was not necessary. They thought the sores would soon be gone. "No," my mother said, "I want her to see a doctor." Amos 3:7 NIV says *"Surely the Sovereign Lord does nothing without revealing his plan to his servants the prophets."*

The next morning Mother, Granny, and I rode to Victoria with Uncle Macon so I could see a doctor. His diagnosis was impetigo, a streptococcal infection that was especially dangerous for me because it was in my nostrils. It could have easily spread, I suppose, through my sinuses to my brain. Left untreated, the impetigo would have continued to spread and would have certainly resulted in damage to my heart. Antibiotics had not yet been discovered.

Because the impetigo was in my nostrils, it was very difficult to treat. The treatment was soaking the scabs in a boric acid solution until they came off. I had to do this with cotton swabs in order to reach way up into my nose. This took much time, patience, and effort, because it was very difficult to get enough boric acid solution into my nostrils to loosen the scabs without breathing the solution into my lungs. After the scabs were finally removed, a sulfur cream was applied to the open sores. Healing would come only with the removal of the scabs and treatment of the infection below them.

Although I begged her to stay with me, my mother had to return to Petersburg that same day. I am sure it was as difficult for her to leave me as it was for me to see her leave. I stayed several more weeks with Granny who helped me treat the strep infection until I was well.

~

"The Lord will keep you from all harm—
He will watch over your life . . ."
—Psalm 121:7—

CAMEO 4

Two Remarkable Visits

All through my childhood I wanted a sister. Mother used to say that she would like to adopt Carolyn, one of the children that I played with at my grandmother's. Carolyn had a twin brother. I remember their mother well. She and my mother became friends one summer in the early 1940s while my mother visited me for a week at Granny's.

Mother was a very friendly person, and she enjoyed going for walks in the country and exploring. I remember one day quite well, because we made two unusual visits. It was a warm summer day, and she and I went for a walk. About a mile or more down the dirt road from Granny's home was the home of the children with whom I often played and watched the cow. Their mother was home alone that afternoon. She was folding clothes when we arrived. I heard her tell my mother that she often had some kind of "heart spells" that caused her to faint.

"The last one I had," she said, "there were angels with me, and I wanted to stay with them. An angel told me that I had to go back this time, but the next time they come, they will take me with them." As we read in Revelation 22:6, *"The angel said to me, 'These words are trustworthy and true. The Lord the God of the spirits sent His angel to show His servants the things that must soon take place.'"*

I heard her tell Mother that she was ready to go! She had washed all of the children's clothes and had them folded. She had food cooked for the family. As we left and walked back down the long driveway from her house to the road, I looked back and saw her pulling dead leaves from a green plant in a hanging basket on their porch. She had on a navy blue dress. That was the last time I saw her alive.

On our way back home to Granny's we passed an old dilapidated, unpainted house of dark aging wood. I would say that it was a well-kept shack. There were flowers around it and large, tall sunflowers in the backyard. The house sat at a fork in the road where we had taken the left fork to my friends' house.

"Wonder who lives here?" Mother asked me.

I told her that Archie Knight lived there. He was an old black man that used to help on the different tobacco farms.

"Let's stop and say 'hello' to him," she said.

"Oh, no, Mother, he is a colored man; we can't go in there," I said.

"Of course we can," she responded, "there is nothing wrong with being colored."

I began pleading with her. "But he works in the yard for us!"

Mother was persistent. "I'm sure he is a nice man and will be happy to see us," she told me as we approached his front door. *"Accept one another then, just as Christ accepted you, in order to bring praise to God" (Rom. 15:7 NIV). ". . . Entertain strangers for by so doing some people have entertained angels without knowing it" (Heb. 13:2 NIV).*

The door was open, and we could see through the almost empty house. He was sitting on the back porch. We walked around to the back of the house and found Archie sitting on the porch drinking a glass of lemonade. He was old, lived alone, and moved rather slowly as he stood up to greet us. His hair was white. His face became one big smile the minute he saw us. Mother greeted him with a warm "hello" and a handshake. She told him who we were. He was obviously pleased to have us visit and immediately invited us to join him on the porch. As we sat down he offered us a glass of lemonade. I timidly said, "No thank you," but Mother, who admitted to being hot and thirsty from our long walk on the dusty road, accepted the lemonade for both of us. As we sat there sipping the lemonade, which was cold and delicious, Mother asked Archie about his flowers. I had never seen sunflowers before. They were really huge and fascinating. Archie told us that sunflowers were his favorite.

"They follow the sun as it moves across the sky," he told us. "I enjoy looking at them during different times of the day. I always have sunflowers in my garden," he said.

It was fun being there with Archie. The three of us laughed a lot as we sipped lemonade on his porch. After a grand visit, we thanked him for our lemonade and bid him farewell.

"Thank you for stopping by to see me," he said. "I enjoyed your visit." His face became one big smile again!

What a special and wonderful day that was! I felt full of joy at having Mother there with me and for the walks, friendship, and love that she had shared with others as well as with me. The visit with Archie Knight was the first time that I remember socially visiting a worker or an African-American. He was more fun to be with than most anyone I have ever known. How he must have loved the Lord! Though he lived in poverty, he had much to share with us. He shared his lemonade, his beautiful garden, and the story of his sunflowers. There was obvious joy in his heart.

From that day to this I have never again felt that I was above or better than anyone. I am neither better nor more blessed. Perhaps I may have had more opportunities than some, but that is all. I thank God for the pleasure of having such a wonderful visit with that dear gentleman, whom He loved. I think of Archie Knight each time I see a sunflower. *"Has God not chosen the poor of the world to be rich in faith and heirs of the kingdom which He promised to those who love Him?" (James 2:5, 6, 8 NIV).*

The next morning we were in the kitchen having breakfast when Carolyn and two of her sisters came to the kitchen door. They were crying. They came to tell us that their mother had died during the night. Later that day, my mother and I went to their house. The children were comforted to hear about what their mom had told us the day before about the angels coming for her and how excited and ready she was to go with them. Stacks of clean clothes and a large pot of soup witnessed to her physical preparations.

Mother went back to their home that night and, while the family slept, she sat with her friend's body until morning. The funeral and burial were the next day.

"How are you lifted up in this cameo?" I asked Him in prayer after writing on a totally different subject than the one I first began. "I am all over the place," I seemed to hear Him say. "I will speak to the hearts of those who read about the visits, and they will see me in different ways."

CAMEO 5

Spiritual Insight

When I was eight or nine years old, I loved to trade jewelry. I had several friends that also liked to trade jewelry, and one summer a friend had a beautiful charm bracelet with Buddhas on it. I was fascinated and thrilled by the bracelet. I don't remember what I traded her for it, but it was something pretty special because I really wanted that bracelet, and she did not want to part with it.

That evening as I held the new bracelet and admired its beauty, I realized that I should not wear idols or have them anywhere in my life, even as charms on a bracelet. Although I had traded for the bracelet because it was beautifully made, the idols ruined its beauty for me. I knew that I should get rid of it. Somehow, the Holy Spirit let me know not to trade it for someone else to wear the idols. With sadness at giving up something I thought was so beautiful,

I destroyed the bracelet. Learning to discipline myself was important. Even though I was not worshiping the idols on the bracelet, I did almost worship the bracelet. It was hard for me to give it up.

Who taught me not to have idols in my life?

First John 2:27 says, *"But the anointing which you have received of Him abides in you, and you need not that any man teach you; but as the same anointing teaches you of all things, and is truth, and is no lie, and even as it has taught you, you shall abide in Him."*

~

*"Those who cling to worthless ideas
forfeit the grace that could be theirs."*
—Jonah 2:8—

CAMEO 6

A Lesson Learned

As a child, I watched with great fascination as Mother or Daddy, depending on whom I was with, lit a cigarette, took a draw, and flipped ashes. When they were not looking, I would sometimes sneak and take a puff off their cigarettes. By the time I was thirteen, I was buying cigarettes and sneaking off alone to smoke. I became quite good at making smoke rings.

When I was thirteen, I took a girlfriend with me for my summer visit to see Aunt Ruth and Uncle Macon at Plantersville. My Grandmother had died when I was eleven years old.

My friend and I played almost every day with a boy our age that lived with his mother across the road nearby. We really had a good time together that summer. We sometimes would go out to the smokehouse and smoke cigarettes together. Ironically, we also played dolls! We also took turns "preaching" at the little church down the road. We had tea parties and went hiking through the woods. We had a wonderful time together! We were settled in for the summer! Before long my girlfriend and the boy we played with each day had a crush on each other.

Suddenly one day I had a terrific urge to "go home" to where my mother lived. I could not get it off of my mind. By late afternoon I was in tears as I told Aunt Ruth that I was homesick and wanted to go home. She told me that if I was awake when Uncle Macon left for work in the morning that my friend and I could ride with him and we could catch a bus from Victoria to Petersburg. I was so afraid that Aunt Ruth wouldn't get us up that I asked my friend if we could take turns staying awake. That way one of us would always be awake and would get the other up in time for us to go with Uncle Macon.

We did not do too well with this plan, although we did take turns for a while. I think Aunt Ruth must have awakened us because we left with Uncle Macon that next morning and traveled from Victoria to Petersburg on a Greyhound bus.

That summer there was a major polio epidemic in our country. It was scary, because it affected many children. Some towns had so many cases of polio that people were asked to roll up their car windows when they drove through the town. At that time no one knew exactly how polio was transmitted, but it was known to be very contagious. A preventive vaccine had not yet been discovered. Many children died and most of those who lived were left paralyzed. My cousin had polio that year and was lucky to be alive. Both legs were left weak and made him prone to fall. I was terrified of polio.

Several days after my friend and I had gone to Petersburg, we learned that our friend at Plantersville had been taken ill three days after we left. He had been taken by ambulance to the Medical College of Virginia in Richmond where he was diagnosed with polio and was in critical condition. I became *very* alarmed. I prayed and thanked God for helping my girlfriend and me leave Plantersville when we did so that we did not play with our friend those last few days before he was rushed to the hospital.

I was so frightened by his illness that I prayed and told God that if He "wouldn't let me catch polio, I would never smoke again!" I meant that prayer with all of my heart. Later in the week, however, without thinking, I picked up my mother's cigarette and took a puff. Immediately, I realized what I had done. I begged for forgiveness; frightened, I went to my Bible, as I often did, and opened it to read whatever the Lord showed me. My eyes focused on a Scripture that taught me that no one can bargain with God. I prayed and continued to ask for forgiveness for not only failing to keep my promise, but also for trying to bargain with God. I told the Lord that I knew that I had broken my promise to Him and that I deserved to get polio. However, I told Him that I would not smoke again for the rest of my life whether or not I came down with polio. I have kept that promise. In my late teen years, when most of my friends began smoking, I still had a craving for cigarettes. It was very hard for me to abstain from smoking. *"I can do everything through Him who gives me strength" (Phil. 4:13 NIV).* I never took even a puff from a cigarette again. When offered one, I learned to laugh and say, "No, I quit smoking when I was thirteen."

What I have learned over the years from this particular event in my life is that God gave me the desire to leave Plantersville that day many years ago. I believe that He protected my friend and me from an environment that may have made us vulnerable to the polio virus.

In addition, through guidance from the Holy Spirit, I learned not to bargain with God. He knew that I was not capable of keeping that promise. I was like Peter who realized this same thing when he heard the cock crow for the third time (Matt. 26:34–35, 75).

What I learned some forty years later, is that cigarette smoking is harmful to the body and causes lung cancer. No one knew that back in those days. God knew that, though, and caused me to give up smoking. He strengthened me for resisting the temptation to smoke. This kept me from an unknown danger, an illness equally as serious as the polio I feared.

God is so good! He is my constant friend, and I love Him with all my heart.

~

"In all your ways acknowledge Him and He
shall direct your paths."
—Proverbs 3:6 NKJV—

CAMEO 7

Envy

As a teenager, I was often envious of my peers. Sometimes I envied a pair of shoes, sometimes a new hairstyle, sometimes a fuzzy sweater or neat skirt. Those things I could usually buy for myself if I really wanted them bad enough, but what would really cause me pain was the envy I felt when a girl had a great personality (which I didn't have) or was dating (going steady with) a terrific guy. Those were the things that I couldn't control, and they almost made me sick. Envy was a terrible part of my life.

One day, when I was in the tenth grade, I was walking down the hall from chemistry class to my next class when I saw a really popular girl who was wearing a fabulous outfit and was holding hands with her handsome, steady boyfriend. Immediately, I became so envious that I could hardly stand it. I knew in my mind that it was good that she had a "bubbly" personality and a neat boyfriend. It was my body that couldn't accept what my mind knew. Envy was, yet again, making me miserable. Although I didn't know it at the time, the "feeling" caused by envy was my physical body's reaction to the pain brought about by being self-centered.

In reality, I had nice clothes and was very pretty. I was extremely shy, however, and lacked self-confidence. Right then, I was miserable seeing this girl with her boyfriend. I did not like those feelings, and I never wanted to feel that way again. I began to pray right there in the hallway as I walked to my next class with dozens of students walking to and from their classes. I prayed as I watched the happy couple hold hands and smile at each other as they walked and talked together. Without realizing it, what I did was enter that inner room of my soul where the Father hears in secret. No one knew I was praying except my heavenly Father who heard my fervent prayer as I asked Him to take the envy away from my life. He answered the prayer immediately. I actually sensed the feelings of envy leave my body. It was a miracle! I could hardly believe it. I was watching the couple again, but now I only felt joy for the two of them. I have never felt envy again. What freedom! What a gift God gave me. He knew how deeply I desired to be free of envy, and He set me free! "*So if the Son sets you free you will be free indeed*" (John 8:36).

⌒

"*He who dwells in the secret place of the most High shall abide under the shadow of the Almighty . . .*"
—Psalms 91:1 NIV—

CAMEO 8

A Reminder

The winter of my freshman year in college, I discovered that most of the girls at school had fur coats. I wanted one too, of course, as having a fur coat was a symbol of affluence and made me feel more acceptable in the "right" circles. I asked my mother to give me a fur coat for Christmas. She agreed to buy one for me for my Christmas and birthday gifts combined (My birthday is on December 31). I was thrilled with having a beautiful fur coat under the tree that year.

Because the coat was important to me, I took great care of it. I enjoyed wearing it on dates, to church, and to many college functions. I liked it so much that I became concerned that I might love the coat too much. I realized that it had become like an idol in my life. I recognized the need to talk with the Lord about this. I prayed to the heavenly Father that I would "get over" the love I had for the fur coat and the need I seemed to have for it in my life.

One night, as I was walking with my date from a fraternity house party to my dorm, we crossed a street where a man was lying after having been struck by a car minutes before. An ambulance had not yet come. It was so cold that I was afraid the man might go into shock. I was taking off my fur coat to put over him when the ambulance arrived. Later that night I realized how pleased I was that I was going to give my coat to the man in need.

After that experience, I often silently asked myself, "Would you give this coat to someone who was cold and needed it for warmth?" As long as I could answer that question with "yes," I enjoyed wearing it.

The Holy Spirit reminded me again not to have idols of any kind in my life.

～

"But the helper, the Holy Spirit, whom the Father will send in my name, He will teach you all things and bring to your remembrance all things that I said to you."
—John 14:26 NKJV—

"I will instruct you and teach you in the way you should go: I will guide you with my eye."
—Psalms 32:8 NKJV—

CAMEO 9

Image of God

$\mathcal{B}$eing a five-foot two-inch brunette who was reasonably attractive, I was fortunate to have lots of dates with terrific guys. The problem was that I only studied enough to make mostly Cs. Unfortunately, I made a D in a clinical course which meant that I had to repeat the course. That meant repeating the entire quarter! Because my grades were mostly Cs, my grade average was lowered by the D, which represented an entire quarter's work.

The dean recommended that I drop out of nursing and go into another field. I was devastated! When I went home for Christmas, I knew that soon I would have to return to school to close my room and take my things home.

Telling Auntie and Unkie was one of the most difficult things I have ever had to do. It turned out, though, that they accepted my news with understanding and encouragement. Auntie insisted that I complete college and get a degree, perhaps at Radford University. The next quarter, though, I stayed out of school to rest and take advantage of an opportunity to spend some time with Aunt Ruth and Uncle Macon who still lived at Plantersville.

Uncle Macon was scheduled to have surgery at the University of Virginia Hospital in early January, and since Aunt Ruth did not drive, they really needed my help. I stayed with Aunt Ruth during Uncle Macon's surgery and his convalescence. It helped both of them that I was available to drive their car while Uncle Macon recuperated at home. Spending this time with them gave me a chance to visit with them and—for the first time as an adult—get to know them better.

As the next quarter rolled around, Auntie insisted that I go back to college. "There is something about that sheepskin that will help you for the rest of your life," she told me. She was definitely right. It helps open many doors in the business world. Since we lived in Radford, going to the University there seemed like the best solution. When I enrolled, I discovered that my class load at Vanderbilt had been very heavy. So heavy, in fact, that even though I had missed a whole quarter visiting with Aunt Ruth and Uncle Macon, I could still graduate with my class.

To develop new interests, I enrolled in a mental hygiene course and took oil painting and modern dance for fun and interest. I was very concerned about taking the mental hygiene course because it was a graduate course. Dr. Thomas, chair of the Department of Psychology, recommended I take it (I am sure with guidance from the Holy Spirit). "With all of the courses you have taken at Vanderbilt," he said, "you will be okay in there."

The course in mental hygiene opened a whole new life for me. As usual, I was continuing to read my Bible each night. Only now, I would learn something in the mental hygiene class during the day and that night would randomly open my Bible and read about the same thing. I quickly found that good mental health and Christianity go hand-in-hand.

What a grand discovery the Lord had provided for me! I soon understood the course so well that Dr. Thomas often called on me by asking, "Miss Townsend, how would you explain that?" Once he asked me what I thought it meant to be made in the image of God. The Lord gave me this to say, "When you look into a mirror you see yourself. The mirror is made in such a way as to reflect your image outward from it. God made our bodies in such a way that His image can be reflected from them. In other words, it is possible for a person to look at another person and see God reflected through their love and actions." After that class I was thrilled when I read Galatians 5:22–23 in the Phillips translation: "*The Spirit produces in human life fruit such as these: love, joy, peace, patience, kindness, generosity, fidelity, tolerance, and self control . . .*"

From that explanation on, Dr. Thomas encouraged me to major in psychology. Following his recommendation and my love for the mental hygiene course, I declared psychology as my major. How wonderful college life had become for me! I still had plenty of dates, but I had gained some sense of how to manage my time, study, and sleep. My first quarter at Radford, I had straight As in all of my courses from oil painting to sociology, which I didn't like but was required to take. My only B was in modern dance. That was not too bad for someone who had only danced socially for fun! As it turned out, that was the only B I made at Radford. All other grades were As, and I graduated with honors.

Another important thing that I had learned was to go to class prepared. I always read and studied the lesson prior to class because I hoped that Dr. Thomas would call on me for an explanation. If he did, I wanted to be prepared. I also went to bed early enough to assure that I would have at least eight hours of sleep so I could think and function at my best. Getting eight hours of sleep had become more important to me than being out on a date. Proverbs 3:13 teaches *"Happy is the man who finds wisdom, and the man who gains understanding."*

For the first time in my life I began to realize that I was an intelligent human being and that I was okay. I wasn't "Rat," as my uncle called me in jest (even though at one time I owned 350 white mice), "ignorant," or "the child," as I was referred to by others. I still had a long way to go, though, before I was truly set free from all those unintentionally hurtful names people near and dear to me used to tease me with, thinking them harmless. Their actions had inadvertently delayed the mental health I so desperately needed.

Often in Dr. Thomas's psychology courses, he would stop in the middle of teaching a specific subject and ask, "Miss Townsend, how would you explain that?" You can never imagine what a boost this was for my confidence and self-image. I had an understanding of the Bible that was new and wonderful, the burgeoning respect of my peers

"But all of us who are Christians have no veils on our faces, but reflect like mirrors the glory of the Lord. We are transformed in the ever-increasing splendor into His own image, and this is the work of the Lord who is the Spirit." (2 Cor. 3:18 PHILLIPS)

∽

and teachers, and the companionship of the the Holy Spirit who guided me to the right school, the right professors, and the right courses. He taught me many new things about Him and about myself. I began to experience a freedom and confidence that I had never known before. After graduating on time with my class, I took a year off to work and think through what I wanted to do. The next fall I returned to Vanderbilt and graduated two years later with a degree in nursing.

CAMEO 10

From Misconception to Light

As an office nurse in a busy internist's office, I saw many wonderful people suffer. A bright spot in the day would be when the doctor's daughter brought in her new baby for a visit. The thought often occurred to me, "How could God make one of these sweet innocent little children pay for the sins of their parents?" The Bible certainly says that children pay for the sins of the parents. I had difficulty understanding a God who would cause suffering to children because their parents had sinned.

Another patient visit that was a happy occasion involved a young woman who came in to get her blood test for a marriage license. A blood test was required in Tennessee to screen for venereal diseases such as gonorrhea and syphilis. Our patient that morning was a beautiful young woman who was the daughter of one of our regular patients. She was very excited about her upcoming marriage. She and her fiancé had been dating several years, and they were very much in love.

When her blood test came back positive, I could hardly believe it. She was going to be declined a marriage license! The doctor came into the lab where I had gone to get the report. I was stunned and concerned about the test. "She doesn't have syphilis," he said. "Her mother had it before she was born, and so it shows up in her child's blood. It will not be easy explaining this to her, though," he said as he took the report into his office.

Children pay for the sins of the parents . . . I could hear that inner voice telling me. God doesn't make the children pay. They suffer because of the sins or circumstances of the parents. Suddenly I had a new understanding. God is good to give us rules to live by. They are important. For one thing, they protect us from various dilemmas; for another, they save us, and they save our children.

Today another example comes to my mind of children killing other children at school. Many authorities believe the young killers have seen so much violence in movies and on television and have practiced so much violence on video games that it has influenced their behavior and caused much of the violence we see today. Who is responsible for teaching such violence? Screenwriters? Movie and television show producers? Who creates the violent video games? My guess is that most of those creators are parents. The children are victims! Regardless of who creates such visual examples of violence, it is parents' responsibility to protect their children from it and teach them to show love to each person with whom they come in contact.

Christian parents have the obligation to teach their children right from wrong and to show kindness and love even to those who may be different in some way from them. Those who need love the most are often the most unlovable. Children can learn to show love and encourage those who need their help. According to one fifth grade counselor who uses a song about bullies and being bullied called "Howard Gray" to reach their young hearts, "This is the time when they're forming identity by identifying with a group and excluding others. They need to learn that you may not like someone, but you have to treat them with respect. You don't have to be mean to one another. We need to start at a very early age." What an opportunity this can provide children, when parents teach them to grow in their relationship with God by calling on the Holy Spirit to help them know how to respond and help others. When you have the opportunity listen to the song "Howard Gray," written more than forty years ago by Lee Domann. It tells the story of a victim of classroom torments and humiliations. It is a wonderful teaching tool.

CAMEO 11

God Is Love

God is Love" is printed in large gold letters above the altar in the little country church that my grandmother founded in 1907. She cut those letters from pages in a magazine and painted them. As a child, I thought that someday I would

Plantersville United Methodist Church, Plantersville, Virginia.
Established 1907.

have enough money to have stone put on the outside of the white wood church and make the altar more beautiful by adding stone to it. I thought that those gold letters up there were too plain. The truth is, I remembered those words all through my life, and I now know that nothing more beautiful could possibly be above that altar.

As a young woman, I was concerned about people in other parts of the world who had never had the opportunity to hear about Jesus. I was even more concerned about those who lived before Jesus was even born. It seemed unfair to me that they had no chance or hope for eternal life. The New and Old Testaments tell us that Jesus is the perfect sinless person and that He died for our sins. What about those poor people that died before Jesus was even born?

"It isn't fair for the truly good people to never have had a chance," I told Him. One day I was praying fervently to Him and begging for an answer to this question. The answer came and when it did it sealed forever those precious words above the altar, "God is Love."

Now that Jesus has been born and has died for our sins, it is of utmost importance that all people accept the wonderful gift of life that He has provided for us. If a person does not accept this gift, then it does not belong to him or her. With Jesus, there is promise for everyone, even for those who are not "loving" individuals. When invited, His Holy Spirit will come into your heart, mind, and body, to teach, guide, and direct you as you live your life through the good times and the bad times. You will receive all you need even through the most tragic and difficult times! *"And my God will meet all your needs according to his glorious riches in Christ Jesus" (Phil. 4:19).*

When you accept Him as a young person, He is with you all of your life as He has been with me. Confessing your sins and accepting Him as your Lord and Savior, even on your deathbed, will bring the promise of eternal life; however, the richness of a full life with Him and freedom of walking in His Spirit during your lifetime on this earth is lost.

To be saved, you only need to confess your sins, ask for forgiveness, and accept Jesus as your Lord and Savior. If you have not done this, and you want to be saved and have the Holy Spirit guide your life, then do it now. Talk to Him as though He is standing right there with you because He really is there. *". . . Repent and be baptized, every one of you, in the name of Jesus Christ for the forgiveness of your sins. And you will receive the gift of the Holy Spirit" (Acts 2:38 NIV).*

He has just given me an example to share with you. My Daddy was a restless person, and he never "complied" to the kinds of things the rest of us did. Opening Christmas gifts was one of those things. Each member of my family loved him and wanted to find that perfect gift to please him. We would shop for hours to find the shirt with a pocket on the left front of the shirt or a sweater with two pockets for his cigarettes and keys. Daddy also liked a certain style sleeve that was hard to find. Shopping for his gifts took a lot of time, shoe leather, money, and love. When at last we had found what we hoped would be the perfect gift for Daddy, we wrapped it special and put it under the tree for him. I really believed, as the Bible teaches, that it was more blessed to give than to receive. I could hardly wait for Daddy to open the gift I had for him. I wanted to see his excitement as he opened the gift that I knew would please him. Yet year in and year out I was disappointed because Daddy didn't always open his gifts with us. "I'll get to it later," he would say. When Daddy died a few years ago, there were still unopened gifts in his drawer.

His last Christmas, I took a great deal of time cutting very thin, lean Smithfield ham to make a sandwich for him. Smithfield ham was his favorite meat, but since he had dentures, it was difficult for him to chew meat. I had practically shaved the ham to provide meat that he could easily chew. I had begged him to come and be with us for Christmas, but he chose not to come. I drove forty-six miles that Christmas Eve just to take him the sandwich to enjoy. When I went back to visit with him and deliver his gifts on Christmas day I saw that he had not even opened the bag that the sandwich was in. When I mentioned that he had not eaten the sandwich, he told me that he couldn't chew ham anymore. He had neither looked at the sandwich nor believed me when I had told him that I had cut the ham thin so he could chew it! I was very disappointed! The sandwich with the wonderful ham was not received.

On a much larger and much more disappointing scale, I know that Jesus must feel great sorrow when His gift of eternal life is not received.

CAMEO 12

Loved

𝒯he phone rang and with excitement I ran to answer it. It was the doctor! "Kick up your heels," he said. "Looks like you will have a new family member in about nine months!"

The love and thrill of having my own home and family was enough to make each day an adventure. Money was scarce during those early years of marriage, and I knew that I must spend carefully and wisely.

The room across from our bedroom would be the perfect location for our little son or daughter. (In those days, not so long ago, there was no way to know even the sex of the baby before birth.) The old curtains, which had hobbyhorses on them, would remain. I would carry out the hobbyhorse theme.

The crib that I bought from a friend was very sturdy and well built. It had great lines but definitely needed a lot of work to make it fine enough to receive our new son or daughter. Other than a small unfinished chest of drawers, the only thing I bought new was a mattress for the crib. I bought the best baby mattress available. Baby's sleep would be restful while his or her little body had the needed support for growth.

It took a while, but eventually a fresh coat of paint brightened the walls and ceiling of the little upstairs bedroom. The paint on the walls matched the color of the hobbyhorses in the curtains.

Preparing for either a boy or a girl, I bought lead-free, child-safe, pink and blue paint along with an antiquing kit to paint the chest of drawers and to refinish the crib. First I sanded the crib to get the old finish off and to remove indentations where three previous occupants had teethed on its edges. Next I painted both the headboard and footboard blue and alternated pink with blue on the side rails. After the paint had thoroughly dried, I applied the antique color over the pink and blue paint and rubbed it off, leaving the deep antique color in the grooves and molding. It looked beautiful—fit for a prince or princess!

Next, the chest of drawers was painted and antiqued blue with the drawers alternating pink and blue. It looked great, and went nicely with the bed. The curtains looked the best they had ever looked, because the entire room—walls, woodwork, and furniture—carried out a hobbyhorse theme with complementary colors.

As I sat on the bare floor admiring my handiwork, I heard a scratching sound on one of the windows. I looked up and saw a limb from the large dogwood tree, which was in full bloom, brushing against the window. It was being moved by a gentle April wind. I leaned back against the wall and watched the beautiful blossoms dance against the windowpane.

As I looked at the petals, each with nail-like imprints, I thought of Jesus on the cross with nails in His hands and feet. The red berries in the center of the blossoms reminded me of His blood shed for me.

For the first time, I began to understand that He really did love me enough to not only die for me, but to actually prepare a place for me to be with Him, much like I was preparing a place in our home for my unborn child.

My baby did not, and could not, do anything to deserve the gift of life. Nor did he or she do anything to deserve the time, money, energy, and love that I had invested in preparing a place for him or her in our home.

Like my baby, I had done nothing to deserve my heavenly Father's gift of life through His Son, Jesus. He loves me anyway!

My mind raced as I recalled the Scripture where Jesus said, "*In my Father's house are many mansions; if it were not so I would have told you. I go to prepare a place for you. And if I go and prepare a place for you, I will come again, and receive you unto myself, that where I am, there you may be also*" (John 14:2 NKJV).

~

"Eye has not seen, nor ear heard, nor have entered into the heart of man the things which God has prepared for those who love Him."
—1 Corinthians 2:9 NKJV—

CAMEO 13

The Remembered Dream

Most dreams leave my mind before I can recall them. But over the years, there have been a few dreams that were so special that they remained in my mind long after the dream. In fact, I cannot forget them. They pop into my mind now and then to remind me of them. I particularly remember one dream that had a significant meaning.

In the dream, I was in the little country church that my grandmother founded. However, before I tell you the dream, let me tell you a bit about my childhood and the church. As a child, I played with friends in the church and often pretended to preach sermons from the pulpit. Once, a boy drove bats from the pipe that ran from one of the two wood-stoves that heated the church in the winter. The two potbelly stoves had been the only source of heat in the church throughout its many years. When Daddy was a young boy, Granny sent him to build fires in the stoves to get the church warm for the Sunday service on cold days. Daddy made a game of it by building hot fires. As they arrived, folks would gather on the benches near the stoves to get warm. Daddy kept adding wood to the stoves and watched as everyone gradually moved away from the heat. It was great fun for Daddy to see how far back the folks would move.

The church was pretty much the center of community life back when Daddy was growing up and later, too, when I was there. Not only did we play in the church, but we also enjoyed ice cream suppers. On special occasions, women in the church brought their best custards and their ice cream makers—the kind where you add rock salt and turn the crank until it barely moves. Oh, the ice cream was good! We also celebrated Children's Day there each year. I always dreaded getting up to recite the poem or verse given to me for my part in the service.

The cemetery was just behind the church. When I was a child, there were only a few graves. Now, there are many. Picnics and homecomings are still held at the church, and food is served on tables set up next to the well-groomed ceme-tery. It is as though we are all, living and dead, there together.

In the dream, I had returned to the church on a Sunday morning. I sat about three rows from the back of the church. I was alone but had left a place between the aisle seat and me. A number of people had gathered in the church, but it was not filled. There were still plenty of empty seats scattered amongst the people. We were all settled in when the church door opened. It was in the back of the church behind me. I turned and looked back to see who had opened the door. It was Jesus. He was dressed in a white robe like I had seen Him in many pictures. My heart nearly stood still. As He came through the door and into the vestibule of the church, it was obvious He had come to attend church too. Oh, I thought, if only He would sit by me! I knew in my heart that He would sit beside someone more special than I. I was just a visitor here today. He walked slowly down the aisle, paused by the bench where I was sitting, and then turned and sat down beside me.

I was thrilled! I could hardly believe that He chose to sit beside me. I smiled and welcomed Him. Then, quietly, I told Him how happy I was that He sat down by me because I had a question that was really bothering me that only He could answer. He leaned over for me to ask Him the question. I asked Him quietly because church had started. He smiled at me and whispered the answer in my ear. Immediately, I understood! It was like a light bulb being turned on in my mind. His answer immediately replaced my concern with joy! It was like a revelation. I now understood the answer to my question. The dream ended.

Later, when I told a Christian friend about the dream, she gasped and said, "What did you ask Him?"

"I don't know," I said, "but it was a question about some biblical truth that I was really pondering over. He made me see it so clearly. There was no need to be concerned over it. I felt such joy and relief."

"Oh, if only you could remember what you asked," she said. I told her that I thought it was much better that I didn't remember the exact question. I think that the answer He gave me was not to worry over things we cannot understand. Someday the answers will be revealed to us as He revealed the answer to my question in the dream. Our concerns will be turned to joy.

CAMEO 14

Gifts Unknown

As a young married woman with a three-year-old son, I was happy and my life was good. Our family went to Sunday school and church almost every Sunday, and together we said our prayers and read bedtime stories each night from a children's Bible. Although my life seemed almost perfect, I longed for something more. I desired a deeper relationship with God.

During that time in my life I happened to read an article written by Billy Graham. He said that his mother always told him that during plateaus in our lives, God is preparing us for a deeper experience. I was definitely on a plateau, filled with the desire for something more! I prayed earnestly that the Lord would give me a deeper experience.

For much of my life I felt that there were words that I should say to someone. Usually they were words of encouragement which I eagerly shared. I loved to encourage people.

But other times I would listen to someone as they talked about a problem or need, and I felt the Lord was directing me to tell them something! I kept asking myself, "Who am I to tell anyone the answer to his or her problems? Much less tell them what the Lord says!"

One day I heard about a Faith at Work conference to be held at Kanuga Conference Center in North Carolina. I really wanted to go. I inquired about it, but there was already a long waiting list and it was only a couple of weeks away. It happened (and I'm sure this was not by chance) that a couple of older friends that I had known from Sunday school called to tell me that they had reservations for the Faith at Work conference and were not going to be able to attend. They wondered if my husband and I would like to go in their place. I didn't even look at the calendar before I said, "Yes."

The conference began on the third of October. My Aunt and Uncle came to stay with our son. The weather was beautiful and warm, and the leaves were brilliant with color. As I went out the front door, my Auntie handed me a coat. "Take this," she said, "you might need it." Obediently, I took the coat, never dreaming that I would need it.

Although my husband was willing to go with me to the conference, he was not especially excited about it. I was so excited that I could hardly contain myself! I knew in my mind and heart that the Lord was taking me on an exciting adventure.

We arrived at Kanuga in time for dinner. Keith Miller was there and introduced his latest book *A Taste of New Wine*. We were assigned to one of the lake cabins. It was rustic, with a fireplace in the living room/porch area. All of us assigned to that particular cabin enjoyed gathering around the fire as the temperature dropped during the early evening. An unexpected cold front was moving in, and the cabin was not heated.

Our room was furnished with two cots. By bedtime it was so cold that my husband and I decided to sleep together on one cot. We combined the two lightweight blankets from each cot to make one as thick as possible. Then, on top of the blankets, we put the coat that Auntie had handed me as we left home. It was colder through the thin mattress underneath us than it was from the top. I slept in my shower cap to help keep my head warm.

Although I am not a morning person, I had signed up for the 5:00 A.M. prayer service in the chapel. When the alarm went off at 4:15, I climbed out of bed, shivering, soon to discover that my makeup was frozen. As I climbed the hill to the chapel, I prayed, "Lord, you have to know that I am serious. I am not a morning person; I am freezing; and I am here only because I love you and want more of you in my life. Please answer my prayer!"

At the conference everyone was assigned to a small group that met together several times during the weekend. I was excited about my small group, and I felt sure the Lord would teach me something there. I certainly prayed that He would. The group leader was a rather prominent seminar leader and speaker for industries and corporations. He greeted us by saying, "I have to be honest with you. I am upset. I was told I would be leading a group of ministers and what I have here is a group of women." So that is how we started our little group.

Guided by one of the most gifted and excellent seminar leaders I have ever known, we began that first evening by introducing ourselves. My heart raced as I told the group my name and made a brief statement about myself. I had always been rather shy, and it was difficult for me to even stand up and tell people my name. During the course of meeting with the group, I shared that with them. We all shared things about ourselves. Then we prayed for each other. In a very short time, we could all feel the presence of God in that room.

One member of the group shared that she had been in a bus station when a poor homeless man had a seizure and fell to the floor. He was frothing at the mouth and his body was shaking and twisting. Everyone moved away from him in disgust. She said she felt no disgust whatsoever as she knelt down beside him, laid her hands on him, and prayed. She said she could feel energy going out from her. The seizure stopped, and soon he was resting quietly on the floor. "Is this real?" I asked the Lord, "or is this lady a kook?" I am a nurse. This is not the medical procedure for caring for someone having a seizure. I had never heard of anything like this before, nor had I heard of some of the other things that this woman shared with us.

On the last night that our group met, the manager of the conference came in to be with us. He had been assigned to our group, but because of his official duties at the conference, he only made this last session. Because he had not had the opportunity to share with us before, we all listened intently as he told of problems in his life. He told us about feeling guilty for not having the time to do many of the things he felt he should be doing for the Lord. He told us some of the things he was doing that filled his time. It was our turn to pray silently for him.

During my prayer, I felt like I should say to him, "God is pleased with you just the way you are. You do not have to change or feel guilty; you are doing exactly what He wants you to do!" Of course I was not going to tell this to the man. Who was I to tell anyone what God thought? At that moment, the woman who had ministered to the epileptic spoke. She said, "God is telling me to tell you that He is pleased with you just the way you are. You do not have to change or feel guilty; you are doing exactly what He wants you to do!"

My heart raced! I couldn't believe it. I was in awe for the rest of the weekend. Many of the things this lady had told us earlier became enormously real and important to me. I now knew that the voice I heard, and had been hearing, was the Lord's voice.

At that Faith at Work conference, I learned there is a deeper spiritual life. One filled with gifts I didn't remember ever having heard about in Sunday school or church. If I had, I certainly had not had spiritual eyes to see or ears to hear. Now Jesus, my intercessor to the Father, had heard my prayers and my eyes and ears were opened. I became acutely aware of His voice speaking to me. At first it was very hard for me to speak out, and I had to force myself to do it. When I pray for direction from Him, He confirms in my mind and heart what I should say. I pray and ask Him that my thoughts will be His thoughts and my words His words.

CAMEO 15

Pearls

For several years, my husband and I played tennis with a small group of friends. Some of them were good players and some, like me, could hardly play at all. Except on one occasion, the best tennis that I have ever played was with a professional tennis player and his wife (who played about like I did). Playing with them was really fun because he would knock the ball directly onto my tennis racket and all I had to do was swing the racket. I looked pretty good playing with them. With everyone else, though, I was not a good player. I missed the ball too much and had trouble serving it.

One night as my husband and I went onto the court, I prayed. "I don't play tennis very well," I said "please, Holy Spirit, you play for me tonight. You live inside me, and I know you direct my life. Please direct my body and play tennis through me." He did! I played tennis like a pro that night. Everyone in the group commented on how well I played! They couldn't believe it. I couldn't either. I was in awe of the situation. I had a priceless pearl.

No one knew that it was the Holy Spirit playing through me. Perhaps I should have told the group that evening how I happened to play so well. But, I choose not to tell them. I believed they would have thought I was crazy.

However, I did tell the Christian group that we worshiped with each Sunday. I explained that I had never experienced anything like it: I didn't miss the ball, and my serves were perfect! It was a wonderful witness to them.

After tennis, we would go to the home of one in the group and have dessert and enjoy being together as friends. It was a terrific group, and we spent many wonderful times together on picnics, as well as the tennis outings each week. No one cared how well the others played tennis; it was really an excuse to get together. We were very informal. Few of us wore tennis white. My husband sometimes did not even wear tennis shoes. The mixture of personalities and talents made the group even more fun. We shared many wonderful times together. Our friendship was like a beautiful pearl.

My friend who originated the tennis group decided one day to invite another couple, whom I knew well, but whom she had just met, to join the group. A red flag went up for me, and I tried to tactfully suggest that they might not fit in with our casual group. I knew from observation and experience that the wife in this couple was a troublemaker, but I didn't speak up as I should have. Instead, I chose to not say negative things about her. My friend said she thought that they would fit in fine and would be a lot of fun to have in the group. I didn't insist against it. These concerns notwithstanding, I liked the couple too. The wife was fun to be around. In fact, she was usually the life of the party. Her husband was a wonderful friend, and I had no doubts about his becoming a part of the group. I knew, however, that his wife usually managed to get people upset with each other, especially women friends.

The new couple joined the group. Within a few weeks, the wife reprimanded my husband for not wearing tennis shoes. The next thing she did was criticize individuals who were not wearing white. This caused several couples in the group to drop out, feeling they were not good enough to stay. Others in the group went to the tennis shop and bought outfits. During the week between tennis matches, this person made phone calls to some to talk about others in the group. She began to criticize those of us who were not good players. She was an excellent tennis player and purposely made most of us look bad. She soon singled out a husband of one of the players and went after him, upsetting the wife, of course. Within a year, this wonderful little group of friends who played tennis as a healthy and fun way to get together, gradually one-by-one abandoned the weekly get-togethers. The tennis group disbanded.

Distinguishing between spirits is called discernment and is one of the gifts of the Holy Spirit (1 Cor. 12:10). If only I had realized that my concern was a gift and listened with my spiritual ears, I would have accepted this gift of knowledge. If I had shared both gifts with my friend, her decision to include this individual in our tennis group may have been a different one and this cameo may have had a very different ending. The point that I am being led to make here is that evil destroys. The evil one used this woman to disrupt a loving group of people. Had we stayed together, I do not doubt that I would have been given the opportunity to tell them, either as a group or individually, about tennis with the Holy Spirit that evening! We will never know the value of those tennis friends as a group, loving, caring, and sharing with each other.

CAMEO 16

Miracle in the Kitchen

*I*t had been a busy day, and during the afternoon my head began to hurt. As the day progressed, so did my discomfort. By dinnertime, I had a full-blown migraine headache.

My son, three years old at the time, was playing in the kitchen while I cooked dinner. He had seen me sit down a time or two and hold my head. As he and I were setting the table for dinner he asked, "What's wrong, Mom?" I told him that for some reason my head was hurting. He came to me and kissed my forehead, "I'm sorry," he said.

After we finished setting the table, he went back to his playthings while I tended the meat cooking on the stove. By this time, my head was hurting so badly that I was almost sick. I was going to have to lie down as soon as I turned the meat and added the rest of the ingredients to the pan. As I stood in front of the stove, adding the ingredients, my head suddenly stopped hurting. It was such a profound happening, that I was almost stunned by the relief. I was so relieved and amazed that I turned to look around the kitchen, as if expecting to see something unusual.

My son was standing behind me with his eyes closed. He was praying. I bent down and hugged him. "Are you praying for my head to stop hurting?" I asked. "Yes," he answered. "Thank you," I said. "My headache is gone and Mom feels great!" We thanked God together for healing my head. Then my son went back to his toys, and I returned to the stove to finish cooking dinner. I silently praised and thanked God for the faith of my son and that miracle in our kitchen.

CAMEO 17

Checkertab

Just before Easter, my husband, four-year-old son, and I were in a feed store shopping for fertilizer and other items for our yard. As we went into the store, we could hear baby chicks cheeping. Our son was excited and ran over to see them. They had been dyed different colors for Easter and were as cute as could be. He and I stayed there watching the chicks while Dad shopped for items we needed for the yard. When he had finished shopping and was ready to leave for home our son did not want to leave the chicks. "May I take one home?" he asked.

Knowing that chicks that have been dyed often do not live long, we discouraged him, explaining to him that a chicken would be a lot of trouble and would be hard to take care of. With his excitement and insistence, however, we gave in and let him choose a baby chick. Selecting one was not an easy task for him. They were all cute and precious. He finally selected a little green one that the salesman put into a box with holes in it for us to take home.

On the way home, we discussed what to name the chick. Of course, we did not know if the chicken would grow to be a hen or a rooster. Dad told us that when he was a child, his family had chickens, and the chicken feed that his family bought in sacks was named Checkertab feed. "Let's name it Checkertab, after the chicken feed," he said. "That will work for either a boy or a girl chicken." We all liked the name Checkertab, so the chicken now had a name.

When we got home, Dad converted a large box into a "room" for Checkertab. He went all out, taking an empty tennis ball can and putting a small electric light bulb in it to be Checkertab's "mom." We padded around the can and Checkertab snuggled up to it, cheeping excitedly. Soon we learned that Checkertab never wanted to be out of sight of one of us. It was only when we went to bed at night and turned out the lights that Checkertab was content with only the "mother" heated tennis ball can.

Often when I was in the kitchen cooking a meal, I would carry Checkertab in his box into the kitchen with me. He would be content in the box as long as he could see me but he would cheep very loudly if I disappeared from his sight.

Our son was gentle and loving to the chick. He would sometimes let Checkertab out of his box to run around. Of course, Checkertab followed our son like he was the mother hen. Our son thought this was great!

One Sunday afternoon, while running in the dining room with Checkertab chasing him, our son accidentally tripped and stepped on the little chicken's leg and broke it. When he saw that Checkertab was unable to stand up, he broke into tears calling me to come quick. I ran to the dining room and there was Checkertab with a broken leg. "It will be okay," I said. "Go find your Daddy." My son, in tears, ran to find his Dad while I wrapped Checkertab in the clean dishtowel I was holding. Dad was soon there to hold Checkertab and help evaluate the leg. Our son was there beside him. As they observed the broken leg, I ran to the kitchen and called the veterinarian. I explained to him what had happened and asked him what could be done to treat the leg. "We will bring the chicken to your office," I said. He laughed and told me there was nothing that he could do for a leg that tiny. You can try splinting it with a toothpick, he told me, "That might work."

I found toothpicks, adhesive tape, and scissors and took them to the living room where Dad was holding Checkertab in the towel. Our son had left the room, and his Dad did not know where he had gone. We slowly opened the towel to look at the broken leg again and try to figure out how to put the tiny splint on it. The leg was no longer broken. There was a trace of blood on the towel, evidence that it had been injured, but the leg was now perfectly intact with no sign whatsoever of having been broken or injured at all. We couldn't believe our eyes. We had seen the broken leg. The chicken had not been able to stand when I had wrapped the towel around him. I immediately ran to find our son to tell him the good news. I called to him and he answered from the half bath downstairs. I opened the door and found him standing in there with his eyes closed. "Are you praying?" I asked. "Yes, I'm praying for Checkertab's leg," he said. "Well, God has answered your prayer," I told him. "Checkertab's leg is not broken anymore. God has healed it!"

Checkertab grew to be a beautiful white rooster with a magnificent red comb.

Max

One rainy morning I was home straightening the house. Max, our German shepherd "asked" to go outside as he usually did in the mornings. It was his habit to go out and stay about twenty minutes and return with a "let me in" bark at the door.

I was busy making beds when I suddenly remembered that Max was still outside. He had been out for almost thirty minutes. I went to the door and called to him. No Max. That was unusual, especially since it was raining. I went back upstairs and finished making the beds. I began crying with tears running down my cheeks. I was startled by this and was surprised that I was crying. Then, without knowing why, I panicked.

I went to the door again and called and whistled for Max. There was no answer and no doggie. I put on my raincoat and got an umbrella. Out in the yard I called and called for Max. There was no sign of him. Our home was on a hill of approximately twenty-six acres. A grand place for a German shepherd to roam. But Max never liked to be out in the rain.

I walked down our driveway, which was about a quarter of a mile long, calling for Max. When I came to the highway at the foot of the driveway I looked in both directions to see if I could see him. I prayed that a car had not struck him.

The entrance of our next-door neighbor's driveway began beside ours. Their driveway was very long also and led into the woods and up a slight hill to their home. As I walked down their driveway, whistling and calling "Max," I stopped by the fence to pet Maurice, their daughter's horse who came to the fence to greet me. I asked Maurice if he had seen Max. I was crying and whistling at the same time. There was noise from the highway, and I wasn't sure, but I thought I heard Max bark. Listening, I kept calling and walking down their driveway where I thought I might have heard him bark. I didn't hear him again, and I wasn't sure I had heard him the first time.

After returning home in tears I kept praying that Max was all right and that he would come home soon. Suddenly, I went to the phone and called our neighbor who lived on the hill, two driveways down from ours. I didn't think anyone was home this time of the morning. The judge and his wife were busy people.

When the judge answered the phone, I was surprised. "Lon, this is Donna," I said. "Max has disappeared. Would he by any chance be at your house or where you can see him?" "I've just walked in the door to pick up something and am on the way back to the office," he said. "I don't think he's here, but I'll look around before I leave." About ten minutes later, the phone rang. It was the judge. "Is Max home yet?" he asked me. "No," I answered. "Well, you will be seeing him in a minute," he said. "He had fallen into our swimming pool and couldn't get out. I had to pull him out. He took off running so you'll see him soon." I couldn't thank him enough!

I ran downstairs and opened the front door. Max was just arriving. He ran by me, ran up the stairs and collapsed in the bathroom beside the tub, his usual place to sleep. He was soaking wet, shivering and gasping for breath. I put a warm blanket around him and stayed with him until he was warm and resting comfortably.

God answered my prayer in a wonderful way. I probably did hear Max bark that one time, but if I had found Max in the pool, I doubt that I could have gotten him out. He weighed about 75 pounds, and I weighed 108 and was not a good swimmer. Instead, God sent my neighbor home for something, alerted me to call at the moment he arrived at home, and caused that wonderful man to look out of the window facing the pool where he saw Max.

CAMEO 19

Lent: "Giving Up" Gifts

I have always thought that the Lenten season is a time for giving up something that is important to me; something like going to the movies or not eating desserts. To my surprise, the giving up of something important to me went deep into my spiritual being, and it required help from the Holy Spirit to succeed. As I gave up that something for the Lord, He replaced the area where it had existed with wonderful gifts of knowledge and wisdom.

While in college, I decided to give up something for Lent. It would frequently remind me of Jesus' love for me.

I thought and thought about what to give up. I finally decided to give up desserts. The university cafeteria had wonderful desserts, and I had a sweet tooth. At dinner each evening during Lent, I passed up desserts and thanked Jesus for loving me.

Many years later, I felt the Lord wanted me to give up something for Lent. As before, I began thinking of things that would be difficult to do without. I still had that sweet tooth, and so, again, I decided on desserts. I didn't think to ask the Holy Spirit what He would have me give up.

The first evening of Lent my family and I ate at Piccadilly Cafeteria. As I went by desserts, I reached for one. Then I remembered I had given up desserts, so I quickly withdrew my hand and began to move on down the line. At that moment, a small, quiet voice inside of me said, "Go ahead, Donna, get dessert, that's not what I want you to give up."

Let me tell you that was an exciting evening in my life! As I ate dinner and dessert, I began to pray that the Holy Spirit would show me what to give up. What He said to me was, "I want you to give up anger." (I heard this with my spiritual ears.)

I was a very patient person. I had a lovely home, a husband, a son, and a part-time career teaching nursing at a nearby university. I had to pray for the Holy Spirit to show me where I was angry so I could give it up. I just honestly didn't feel that I was angry.

He answered that prayer! The next day, as I sat at my desk thinking, I slowly began to realize that I harbored a great deal of anger toward my husband. As I became aware of my anger, I also became aware that I could not, on my own, give it up. The situations causing my anger were real, and I could not change them.

I felt trapped! I was angry and had not known it. I was powerless to change the situations causing my anger. Anger was justified, but anger was keeping me from experiencing much joy available to me.

Without the love and instruction of the Holy Spirit, I would have been lost in anger without ever even realizing it!

Again, I prayed for help. I told Jesus, "I want to give up anger . . . and if You want me to give it up, You will have to show me how to do it. I cannot do it on my own."

Over the next few days, I began to understand the behavior that triggered anger in me. Gradually, I learned of one situation after another from my husband's childhood that contributed to his personality and behavior. I remembered that he had told me that when he was a boy he had wanted to be a Boy Scout, but his father went to bed at 7:00 P.M., the time the troop met, so he couldn't be a Boy Scout.

He also had wanted to be a student patrol boy, but because his sister couldn't be ready for school that early in the morning, his parents would not let him be a student patrol boy either.

We lived in the house where he had grown up. I suddenly realized that his room, which was next to his sister's, had received only one coat of paint in over twenty-five years. It was the original paint!

His sister's room, however, had been painted two times and had, in addition to the paint, four layers of wallpaper. No wonder he had free-floating anger! It was usually directed at our son and me!

During this time, when I began to see what I had not seen before, my husband happened to mention that when he was a child, he had wanted a new desk like his sister had. His parents brought up an old radio from the basement and put a door across it to make a desk for him. "It was okay," he said "it served the purpose."

His sister received a scholarship for college, and at her request, their parents gave her the money they would have spent for her education.

My husband received a scholarship for college also, but he was not given the money from his parents. I asked him why. His answer was, "Didn't ask for it. I figured they would have given it to me if they had thought I deserved it." His self-worth was damaged at every turn!

As the Holy Spirit helped me to understand my husband's past, I was able to let go of my anger. The situations triggering anger did not change, but my understanding had changed, and my life changed and became better. By gaining insight and understanding into my husband's past, I could be more patient with him. My spiritual eyes allowed me to see beyond the hurtful behavior so that I could respond with love.

"Trust in the Lord with all your heart and lean not on your own understanding."
—Proverbs 3:5 NIV—

CAMEO 20

Fear

$\mathcal{I}$ had a dear friend that was a very successful business-woman but who lived in constant fear. She feared she would make mistakes on big business deals and clients would find out that she wasn't the most savvy businessperson. She feared that she was a failure as a daughter, sister, wife, mother, and friend.

I thought that if I had perfect love for her it would cast out her fear. I kept praying for more perfect love, and I tried every way I knew to show love to this friend, who had accomplished much good through her business and as a children's rights advocate in the community. She simply did not believe that she was okay. She felt undeserving and guilty. Her guilt went way back to childhood. She was like a coffee cup that has a crack in it and can't hold coffee. She could not accept love from the many that loved her.

One day, wanting so desperately for her to be free of fear, I was praying for more perfect love to show her when I heard that still small voice say to me, "Donna, perfect love does cast out fear. But for love to cast out fear, love must replace fear in the fearful person. Love replaces the fear leaving no room for fear. Your friend must be willing to accept the love." In other words, she had to invite that perfect love of Jesus into her life in order to be free of fear. What freedom I gained from that marvelous revelation! Thank you, Holy Spirit, for teaching me!

∽

"There is no fear in love. But perfect love drives out fear,
because fear has to do with punishment. The one who
fears is not made perfect in love."
—John 4:18—

CAMEO 21

An Adventure with the Holy Spirit

God had placed me on the Spiritual Formation Committee of our United Methodist Church. I feel certain that He placed me there because I was open to the leading of His Holy Spirit. Although our church had over two thousand members, there were only seven of us on the committee. Our job was to plan workshops, seminars, and speakers during the upcoming year to give spiritual strength to our membership.

At our first meeting, Dr. Ross Whetstone was mentioned as an excellent seminar leader. We had information on one of his workshops entitled "Clothed with Power." Although I had not heard of him, someone in the group had attended one of his workshops and thought he had excellent content material and presentation skills.

We discussed several other opportunities, but after looking over the brochure for "Clothed with Power," we all thought this workshop would be the most helpful and inspirational for our church members. Dr. Whetstone was serving as executive director of the United Methodist Renewal Services Fellowship, UMRSF for short, now known as Aldersgate Renewal Ministries (ARM). We soon had a date scheduled for "Clothed with Power."

In early fall when Dr. Whetstone arrived, our committee members met with him during dinner before the first session began. I liked him immediately. He was full of spirit, laughter, and conversation.

"Clothed with Power" was excellent. The only disappointment was the number of people who did not attend. Only about fifty of our two thousand-plus members were there. I am certain, however, that the individuals who did attend were those that were truly searching for something more, and the Lord led them to the "Clothed with Power" workshop. This was certainly true in my case, and in a way far more significant to me personally than I could have dreamed at the time.

On Sunday morning, just before the church service in which Dr. Whetstone had the main address, the committee member assigned to take him back to the motel after church asked me if I would take him for her. Something had come up, and she needed to be free to take care of that. I said, "Yes, of course."

It was a delight to have that special opportunity to talk with Dr. Whetstone. Actually, an opportunity to talk with him on a one-on-one basis was an answer to my prayer. A month earlier, I had received a call to go into the ministry, and I was struggling to know God's plan for me as a minister. I had hoped to talk with Dr. Whetstone about it.

As he got into my car, I knew immediately that the Lord had arranged this special time for me. I shared with Dr. Whetstone that I felt led to go into the ministry and had talked with my pastor and district superintendent about it. "They think I should go to divinity school," I said. "I have applied and been accepted to Candler at Emory University and Perkins at Southern Methodist University. I don't think I am to preach, though," I told him, "but perhaps write or minister in some other way." As we neared the motel, Dr. Whetstone asked me if I had time to eat lunch with him. I did have time, and we talked two hours over Sunday brunch.

He asked numerous questions and listened intently as I answered. He told me that what I knew, I might never learn in divinity school. He encouraged me to continue to be open and to follow the leading of the Holy Spirit. God not only provided that opportunity for me, but began placing me where He wanted me to become involved in ministry in a new and special way.

That was in November 1988, and was the real beginning of finding my place in the ministry for which the Lord had been preparing me all of my life.

In January of the next year, I was invited to attend a two-day praise-and-worship meeting of the UMRSF board and council in Nashville in February.

What a wonderful experience it was! I drove my car to Nashville and arrived there Thursday afternoon in time to have dinner with a dear friend, with whom I stayed for the weekend.

That first evening with the UMRSF group was remarkable. The twenty to twenty-five beautiful individuals who gathered there were a wonderful and interesting group of people. They came from all over the country and, like me, loved the Lord. We were asked to form a large circle and hold hands as Dr. Whetstone opened the first session with a prayer of thanks and anticipation of our time together with the Holy Spirit. Then we introduced ourselves to each other and told a little about ourselves.

My eyes focused on each person as I looked around the room. Suddenly, something inside of me became critical of almost everyone there. This was *not at all* like me! "She looks like she might play a tambourine on a street corner," I thought. "All he needs is a gun and a pair of boots." "She doesn't look like she could possibly know anything." "He would make a good street beggar." "She talks too much to listen." "He looks like he doesn't have sense enough to come in out of the rain." I had a critical thought about nearly everybody in the room.

After introductions, we sang praise songs. Most of them I had never heard, but they were very beautiful.

Tears flowed from my eyes as we praised God and worshiped Him. One man felt that the Lord had given him a verse to share with the group. We all turned to the place in the Bible as he read the Scripture. I don't remember which Scripture it was, but it was a perfect message from God that related to our weekend and the work that we accomplished. There was a prophecy too. My excitement grew as I recalled the wonderful Sundays (as related in

"Understanding the Prophesy"), many years ago, when the teachers came from Canada to teach our small group in homes. There we had praised God with arms held high as songs and prophecies flowed. Now I was experiencing the same joy as then. I felt like I was *home*. Only this time, it was with a small group of United Methodists, and God had placed me with them.

Dr. Whetstone then gave a brief report of his travels and workshops over the past few months and provided us with an overview of the weekend. As we finished our first evening together, he asked a very pretty lady in the group to give our closing prayer. Immediately I thought, "Why is he asking her? What kind of a prayer can she pray?" The lady began praying one of the most beautiful prayers that I have ever heard. I was amazed!

On my way back to my friend's house, I prayed fervently and asked God to take away the critical spirit that had swept over me at the meeting. "You know I am not like that, Lord. I am not a person who is critical of others. Why was I like that tonight? It was a wonderful evening, Lord," I said, "and I thank you for bringing me here." I begged His forgiveness for looking at some of the people and judging them by outward appearances. Then I heard His voice, "Tonight you saw individuals as the world sees them. Tomorrow I want you to look at each individual and see Me. Look into their eyes, listen to what they say, and recognize Me."

What a thrill it was for me to hear the voice of my Lord! What a wonderful assignment He gave me that night. The next morning, I eagerly arrived at the meeting and began looking for Jesus in each person. He was there! I now look for Him in everyone I meet.

When I see Him in others, I cherish the opportunity to share with them my love for the Lord. What wonderful conversations

I have had with some of the most unlikely people! Oh, for the opportunity to again visit with Archie Knight and learn more about Jesus from his life with the Holy Spirit.

～

"I heard a shout from the throne saying, 'Now the dwelling of God is with men, and He will live with them. They will be His people, and God Himself will be with them and be their God.'"
—Revelation 21:3 NIV—

CAMEO 22

The Shells

Several years before my marriage of twenty-eight years ended, I knew it could not continue in the state it was in. I had done everything I knew to do. I prayed constantly for help and guidance. I was grieving, angry, and in despair.

One evening, my best friend from college, whom I had not heard from in several years, called and invited me to join her and two other friends, former classmates, for four days on Captiva Island at the newly purchased beach house of one of the girls. I said, "YES!" What a wonderful four days awaited me!

The first morning that I was there, I went out on the beach alone to walk and think. I prayed and asked the Lord to teach me something through a shell. Then I set about looking for that special shell. The first one to catch my eye was a white delicate little shell that reminded me of a bridal veil. I gathered several of these (all alike), but there was no special message that came to me through the shells. I decided to look for another kind of shell; I looked through a group that had just washed up on the shore, and a tiny shell that looked like the Clemson Tiger paw caught my eye. I washed the sand from the shell and studied it carefully. When no message and no special thought came to me, I put it in my pocket along with the first shell. I will just keep them, I thought. Since no messages had come, I began to pick up interesting and pretty shells to keep in a collection.

Marcelene, one of my friends, and the only one of us that was from Florida, walked up beside me and said, "Oh, you've found some shells, let me see if I can name them for you." There was a lady's slipper, a turkey wing, a baby's cradle, and several others that she named. I then took the two from my pocket and said, "Tell me what these are." "Oh," she said, "this one is a baby's foot" (the first shell I had chosen). Picking up the second shell in my hand she said, "This second one is a lion's paw."

Later, when I was alone, I studied the two shells that I had been led to pick up—the baby's foot and the lion's paw. As I studied them I could hear that still small voice say to me, "You must step out in weakness as on a baby's foot, but I will strengthen you like a lion."

I could hardly contain my joy! I knew the Lord had answered my prayer. He had also confirmed that He was with me. Second Corinthians 12:9–10 says, *"My grace is sufficient for you: for my strength is made perfect in weakness. Most gladly therefore will I rather glory in my infirmities, that the power of Christ may rest upon me. Therefore I take pleasure in infirmities, in reproaches, in necessities, in persecutions, in distresses for Christ's sake: for*

I showed her the two shells in my pocket.

when I am weak, then am I strong." Isaiah 41:10 says, *"Fear not; for I am with you: be not dismayed; for I am your God: I will strengthen you; yes, I will help you; yes, I will uphold you with the right hand of my righteousness."*

I had no idea of the intensity of the pain and heartache that was soon to follow through betrayal, divorce, and the death of my Auntie whom I loved like a mother. My sense of loss was almost overwhelming. I became almost too weak to function. Each step I took was in weakness.

Often, in the middle of the night, I would awaken and feel the pain of loss, anxiety, hurt, and bitterness. I knew I was not filled with the fruit of the Spirit. I would pray and ask the Holy Spirit to help me overcome all of my negative feelings. My prayer became this: Lord Jesus, I can't love this man who has betrayed me. He has caused me so much pain. Jesus answered and said to me, "I know how you feel. I too was betrayed!" "Jesus," I asked, "how did you keep on loving those who were killing you?" He answered, "Because I could see them as they really were. They were blind to the truth. They did not know what they did." Then I prayed, "Please let me see this man as you see him. Let me love him with your love, because I can't love him on my own! Empty me of those things that are not of you and fill me with your love." My constant prayer became this: "Please help me to see him as you see him. Help me to love him with your love and please *don't let him hurt me anymore.*"

There were times when I just wanted to get even, but instead I prayed that my husband would come to know Jesus as his personal Lord and Savior. I hoped that he would be released from anything that would keep him from becoming the person God created him to be. With the help of the Holy Spirit, I came to realize the impact of this prayer. The more love that each of us has within us, the better our relationship to each other and with our son. My physical body did not want him to have the love and salvation that I had, but on my spiritual level, I knew that if he had what I had then I would be secure and the two of us could work together for the good of all involved.

God is so good! He has answered my prayers and His love has strengthened me as a lion. The Lion of Judah!

⁓

"Then one of the elders said to me 'Do not weep, see the Lion of the Tribe of Judah, the root of David, has triumphed . . .'"
—Revelation 5:5 NIV—

CAMEO 23

A Cold November Afternoon

A few days before Thanksgiving, I eagerly awoke at Jim and Lynnie's home, where I often stayed during the last months of separation from my husband. I knew I would be leaving as early as possible to travel to Louisville to visit my friend from college and her wonderful husband who was dying from Lou Gerhig's disease. After visiting my friends for one night, I planned to travel on to Clarksville, Tennessee, to spend Thanksgiving with my sister and her family.

I packed my suitcase, put clean sheets on the bed, and straightened my room so Lynnie would not have much to do to prepare for the incoming guests who would be staying there. Lynnie and Jim had taken me in like a daughter during the weeks before my divorce. My friends' grown children and grandchildren were coming for the holidays, and a big family reunion was planned. I knew they would be happy for me to be there too, but I wanted to visit my friends and be with my sister and her family for Thanksgiving.

It was very cold that day and snow was predicted, so I had to get snow tires before I left. As I left for the tire appointment, I told Lynnie and Jim good-bye and gave them a warm hug. We wished each other a "Happy Thanksgiving."

It was nearly 4:00 P.M. by the time the new tires were on my car, ready for me to take my trip. There was some snow locally and on the roads ahead as well. However, the roads were still relatively safe for travel. I had to decide if I wanted to travel over the mountains at night, alone, with the temperatures dropping into the teens. I decided to wait until the next day to leave. Instead of returning to Jim and Lynnie's house, I went instead to our home where my husband was living. I didn't mind being there for the night as he was on a two-day trip. I had not moved out, but there was a great deal of friction to say the least and I was temporarily staying with friends. When I arrived home, I discovered the house was cold. The electrical system that fueled the furnace with oil was broken. It was too late in the day to reach anyone who could fix it.

I turned the oven on to help heat the kitchen and closed the kitchen doors to the rest of the house. While the oven began heating, I pulled up a chair and sat in front of it with the oven door open. I sat there shivering with my coat on praying as to what I should do. The temperature was in the low twenties outside. I was tired, and there was really no place comfortable to sleep in the kitchen. I will have to sleep here, I thought.

As I sat there praying, I felt disappointed at not being able to have left early in the day. I did not want to go back to my friends' home for the night and interfere with their Thanksgiving plans. I was really scared to sleep in the kitchen with the oven on all night. I continued to pray. I had been talking to the Lord all day, and now I was asking Him to help me know what to do in this scary situation.

The phone rang while I was praying. It was a friend that I had known during the summers when we stayed and played at our place on the lake. She and her husband had a lake house close to ours. Her husband had died, rather young, several years ago. We had never been close friends, and I had only seen and talked with her casually over the years. "Donna," she said, "it is such a cold night. I have made a big pot of soup and built a fire in the fireplace. I just wondered if you would come and have some soup and spend the night with me?"

I am not surprised anymore when God answers my prayers, sends someone to me, or guides how I think or what I do. It does, however, *always* thrill me when He does it in such an obvious way as this! "Peggy, you are an answer to prayer," I said. "My bag is already packed, and I would love to share your soup and spend the night with you!"

She gave me directions to her home and was waiting at the door when I arrived. We spent a wonderful evening together sharing many experiences of how the Lord helped us through difficult times. We said good-bye as we went to bed that evening because I wanted to leave very early the next morning. I set my clock and slipped out as planned without waking her.

⁓

"Have I not commanded you? Be strong and courageous. Do not be terrified; do not be discouraged, for the Lord your God will be with you wherever you go."
—Joshua 1:9 NIV—

CAMEO 24

My Song

$\mathcal{I}$ began singing this little prayer which came to my mind as I drove alone over a Virginia/Tennessee mountain highway in

1989 on my way to meet clients. This was during a *very* difficult time in my life:

> Lord Jesus, be with me today
> In all that I do and all that I say.
> Hold me close and fill my heart
> With your wisdom, your words, your love
> To impart
> To all I see who have a need
> Which you can meet through me.

~

*"Don't you know that you, yourselves are God's temple
and that God's Spirit lives in you?"*
—1 Corinthians 3:16 NIV—

*"Whatever you do, work at it with all of your heart,
as working for the Lord, not for man."*
—Colossians 3:23 NIV—

CAMEO 25

God's Gift

𝒟ivorce is terrible! To know that the one I loved and chose to be my life mate was unfaithful, didn't love me anymore, and wanted a divorce was devastating! Along with this realization, I knew that life could never be the same. I would no longer live in the home I had known as mine for twenty-eight years. I would no longer own the bridle path that I loved so much, the path that made a complete circle around the hill where our home was located.

In the winter, it was great fun to walk around that bridle path's approximate mile. There was a river below a cliff in the rear of the path. From several locations, I could look up through the leafless trees and see our home on the hill in the distance. When it snowed, this path became more exciting than ever. I stepped carefully to avoid disturbing the precious tracks of rabbits that traveled parts of the circle earlier that morning. I liked imagining where they were going. The path became a winter wonderland. It was thrilling to see the tall trees standing majestically draped in white. There was a lot of excitement in the woods as I walked in the winter. The birds flew anxiously through the air looking for something to eat. Their songs were music in the world as they praised our heavenly Father and thanked Him for the many berries available to them.

In the spring, this path was filled with dogwood and redbud trees full of blossoms. An albino redbud grew by the path. Its white blossoms intrigued me year after year. The pear trees also had blossoms. There were apple trees too, and persimmon. In the spring, the woods were filled with excitement of birds as they gathered small twigs and bits of God's wonderful world to build nests in which to lay their eggs. Small animals scurried to do who-knows-what while they, too, felt the excitement of spring in the air!

Summers were a little difficult. On the first walk of the day, one had to carry a stick to remove spider webs where they had been spun across the path to catch insects flying toward the sun's light as it streamed through the trees. Summers were hot and muggy, but the activity and beauty of the world as seen from the bridle path was worth the discomfort of webs and summer heat! The trees were tall and lush with leaves. There was delicate fern growing in moss along the path and mingled in it were many different kinds of wild flowers. Sassafras roots, which make wonderful tea, were available with a little digging. I was thrilled as I praised God for this beautiful path, which, though hidden from view, was actually a major part of our yard! How fortunate I was to witness the beauty and life along the path!

It was summer when our son, our German shepherd dog, Max, and I had picnics together. Along with a small picnic cloth, paper plates, and a paper bowl, we took peanut butter and jelly sandwiches and a packet of special dog food. The three of us would head for the bridle path and our favorite spot overlooking the river. I would spread a tablecloth, and lay out paper plates for our sandwiches and a bowl for Max's food. Max would wait patiently as I put our sandwiches on the plates and then poured his food into the bowl. Max continued to wait by his bowl while my son or I said a blessing; then he ate when we ate!

Our son learned to whistle on this stretch of the bridle path. He had tried and tried with sounds coming from his little lips, but not a whistle. It took all summer of the year he was five before he finally came out with a genuine whistle! He was thrilled! I was too! He began whistling at that spot along the bridle path and whistled almost continuously for several years! He whistled in department stores, while he was water skiing, and everywhere he went. People often commented, "What a happy little boy!" or "Listen to that little boy whistle!" His newfound skill had its beginning on a log beside the bridle path. That log, where I often sat while he and Max played nearby, is still there. The years have taken its toll on it though, and it has now become a pile of large splinters.

In the autumn, the leaves turned magnificent colors and fell to the ground making a colorful and velvety carpet for my feet. The squirrels excitedly gathered nuts for winter. They scurried around with tails twitching but became very still as they heard my footsteps through the leaves. In the trees—along with mistletoe and vines of honeysuckle—were large nests where squirrels slept in safety until hunters came and blasted their guns to shoot them from the nests. At home, when we heard hunters shooting, we ran to the balcony of our bedroom and shouted as loudly as possible, *"No hunting!"* If gunshots continued, we called the police. After they found our bridle path, folk from nearby residential areas seemed to think it was okay to hunt in our woods. Although most of our twenty-six acres were wooded, we were in the city, and this was our yard. How fortunate I was to know this beautiful spot so well and to have the opportunity to observe the interesting myriad of activity that went on there.

It was autumn of my life too! I was fifty-three years old, and my husband wanted a divorce. The lovely autumn day was cool and crisp. My jacket gave just enough warmth as I began the mile walk alone around the bridle path. Memories of so many years of wonderful and happy times brought tears. My loss was devastating! As I took the hand of the one I had always counted on, I cried out to Him. "Dear God, I can't stand this! How can I live without owning this bridle path? I can't stand it if my husband owns this bridle path, and I can no longer be here!" He answered me! His voice was gentle and firm. "Your husband doesn't own this bridle path, nor did his parents before him, nor the Indians before them! I own this bridle path; it is mine. I have other places more beautiful than this to take you."

There was no doubt in my mind that God had spoken to me. I was comforted beyond measure by His words and began to let go of the life I had known for so long and to rest in the love of my Comforter. *"If God is for us who can be against us?"* (Rom. 8:31 NIV).

Four years quickly came and went. One day, I walked down a narrow sidewalk beside the Gulf of Mexico. Seagulls flashed white against the blue sky as they circled above the water looking for fish near the surface of the emerald green sea. Flowers around me presented a radiant array of multi-colors, rivaling only the trees with flaming red blossoms and the Jacaranda trees with their purple.

A new path.

Palm trees blew gently in the breeze. I watched a blue
heron as he fished on the water's edge. He seemed to avoid
getting his feet wet. A white egret landed close by him as if
to watch. It was all so very beautiful! It seemed like para-
dise! I began to praise God for the beauty all around me on
this fabulous island. As I praised Him, I could see my condo
in the distance, much like I once could see my home in the
distance from the bridle path. Suddenly, I realized that I
was now walking on a new path, more beautiful than the
first. God had taken me, as He said He would on that chilly
morning several years ago, to one of His "other places
more beautiful than this."

CAMEO 26

Gift of Time

The year that my divorce became final, I was grieved by
the loss of all those years—twenty-eight to be exact.
During prayer, I told the Lord of this terrible realization of
loss and how I was grieving because of all those wasted
years. While I was praying, it seemed He said to me that He
would make up those lost years, and I would have that time
back. This seemed impossible to me and was almost
beyond my ability to believe. How wonderful it would be if
that happened.

During an Aldersgate conference later that same year,
a pastor, who did not know of my grief, prayed for me

during an altar call. While praying, she received this prophecy for me: "God will give you back the time which you have lost."

God is so good! I have had more time than ever before. Somehow, I seem to do so much, that I can hardly believe that only a week has gone by, or only a year. This gift of time has been another miracle in my life. Years later a friend gave me a Scripture which may relate to the prophecy.

⁓

"I will repay you for the years the locusts have eaten . . ."
—Joel 2:25 NIV—

CAMEO 27

Journaling

Journaling is something that I have known about for many years, and I believe it has many merits. It gives an individual an opportunity to put their thoughts down on paper; it provides a wonderful record of the progress one makes through life. Journaling has been difficult for me because it takes time and effort to sit down and actually write. Believe it or not, I used to hate to write. At least, I did when it had to be done the old-fashioned pen-and-paper way.

When I was a child, Auntie made me sit down once a week and write a letter to my mother. Today, I am glad she did that, because I know those letters meant a great deal to

Mother. She had saved many of them, and I found them after her death. I always dreaded to write, though, because fortunately for me, Auntie made me do it correctly. This meant that I had to use a pen and ink, spell each word correctly, and, if I made a mistake, I had to use a razor blade to gently scrape the mistake off the page (correction fluid had not been developed) and then add the correction. This "torture" began when I was in the first grade and was just learning to form my letters. It took *great* effort on my part. It took a lot of time sitting there and forming letters to write what Auntie thought I should say. It was easier later when I had my own thoughts to share with Mother. I later learned that if they were negative, they were never mailed. I found some of the letters I had written as a child after Auntie died. She had saved them for me to read.

Although I took typing in high school, I seldom typed anything after I completed the class. As a result, I did not type very accurately or quickly. Writing something by hand was quicker for me. For term papers in college—and later press releases and reports for my job—I wrote in longhand on a legal pad. I had arrows going from one paragraph to another and asterisks, stars, and all kinds of symbols to let the typist or secretary know where to put different things on the page. My secretary hated getting one of these documents from me!

This is all to say that I did not do much journaling! The counselor, whom I was going to see during the rocky last year of my marriage and year of separation prior to my divorce, suggested it was important for me to write down my thoughts each day. After I had written in my journal, I was to summarize my writings and in a sentence or two, make a brief statement about what I had learned or thought that day. Prior to my divorce, I only wrote a few times in my journal. There were days between my writings. I did not write on any one tablet as I should have nor did I keep the journals in one place together.

There were two days, however, in July 1989 that I did write down the day's events with a short statement about my thoughts for the day. Anyone who has gone through a separation and divorce from someone they love already knows the agonizing pain that haunts life during those difficult times. At first, I felt a pressure on my body. It was like a dark cloud that hovered over me everywhere I went, and it was so heavy on my shoulders that I could hardly move. I literally carried a weight on my shoulders. With almost continuous pleading for help from my Lord, one day I actually felt its weight lift off my shoulders. The relief was more than welcomed. I was still having a terrible time living each day, but I didn't have that terrific weight on my shoulders. I read my Bible each evening when I climbed into bed alone. I was angry, bitter, and grieving, even with my twenty-three-year-old son there some of the time to comfort me. He was a busy pilot, but was wonderful to spend as much time with me as he could. He, too, was grieving over the loss of his family and the stability that a family brings. It bothered him to see me hurting. That night I read Phillipians 4:8 *". . . whatever things are true, whatever things are noble, whatever things are just, whatever things are pure, whatever things are lovely, whatever things are of good report, if there is any virtue and if there is anything praiseworthy—meditate on these things."*

On Monday, July 3, I wrote: Today has been rainy, and I have felt teary-eyed off and on all day. I am concerned about my son . . . . [who was depressed after his dad spoke to him in a tone of disgust earlier today]. I have thought off and on about how good it is now not to be under constant condemnation. Sometimes I have felt rejection, and this brings on tears. I feel a loss for the family and the support of knowing that I have someone to turn to. When I thought tonight (alone, because my son is out of town) about having no one except my son, to care whether I live or die or am happy or sad, I realized that I do have folks who care! My sister and her husband are wonderful to me, as are my niece and nephew. My cousin and his wife care, and they will include me in their lives. If I reach out [here I named several cousins, friends, and relatives], there are many others that need me as well as I need them.

See how the Holy Spirit was coaxing me and making me realize that others needed me.

Earlier today I thought about driving off a bridge and letting my husband have everything, which is what he wants. . . . [More written here about my son and my concern for him, because this is a loss for him as well as for me.]

I talked with [the counselor] tonight. He returned my call of Friday and again earlier today. He said my husband and I shouldn't talk. . . . He wants permission to talk with both of our attorneys to speed the process of dividing assets, etc. He said he would try to make arrangements to be at the hearing (I asked him if he would be there). He sees a special spirit in my husband, as I do, which he hopes to bring to the surface. I'm to call him if I get deeply depressed. Tell whoever answers that it's an emergency. I told him I'm so tired of being condemned. My husband is cruel to me. The counselor has seen this cruelty in him also . . . [We discussed a particular situation]. I am better off without my husband. Short of a miracle, I would be plain stupid to submit myself to such abuse as I have allowed! Had I been more assertive and less tolerant, perhaps his aggressive and moody behavior could have been stopped years ago. . . . Then perhaps his gentle nature could have grown.

Thought for the day: *Do not let the moods of others influence me!*

On Tuesday, July 4, I wrote: Today I worked at home. I washed clothes, dishes, and began working on getting family pictures together. I'm working on [a client's] marketing plan and brochure designs.

I have been a bit tearful. Not bad. Had dinner with [a couple of friends] and we watched a Steve Martin video movie. House is quiet with [my son] not here. I'm very tired, hard to concentrate on the strategic marketing plan. My right eye continues to bother me and my finger joints, especially left hand, are stiff and a bit sore, perhaps from using clippers on shrubs.

No word from [husband] today. I declined a friend's invitation to the lake picnic [annual event of families around our lake house] . . . I am not going to hope for reconciliation any longer. I am making myself accept that my marriage is over, and I will go on with my life. I will pursue the days ahead from this point of view. I will not look back."

Thought for the day: *My marriage is over. I will not look back . . . only to the future.*

Our divorce hearing was the following year on March 10, 1990. The judge ruled on March 20, at which time the divorce became final and was filed.

The above notes were written on one of several legal pads that I used for various notes, records, and memos during that year. They were put away and forgotten.

A wonderful man named Bob came into my life. He had been widowed the year before and needed my friendship and comfort as much as I needed his. After several months, we realized that we cared a great deal for each other. When that caring turned to love, we began talking about a life together. We decided on a wedding date in the fall—a Saturday—so all of our children (he had three and I had one) could be there with us. We signed a contract to purchase a new home, and it would become ours on the first day of November. We began our marriage by living in his home part of the time and my home part of the time while we gradually moved our things into our new home. There was a lot of memorabilia in both of our houses to sort through. Years of "things" had accumulated from the time of the births of our children through their college years and the marriages of his two daughters. We both had unmarried sons.

About two years after Bob and I settled into our new home, I was going through some of the boxes I had kept. In one of the boxes, I came across the notepad with my two days of journaling written there. During the whole year of 1989, I only wrote on those two days in July. I sat there in the floor and read them. The first one reminded me of the terrible depression and agony I suffered. I realized, though, that through writing down my thoughts and feelings that day, I learned two very important truths. First, God showed me that others needed me as much as I needed them and that I should reach out to them. That was hard for me to do, and I didn't feel like it, but I did it, and it helped me immeasurably. Second, He made me realize that

I must not let the moods of others influence my own. That took some renewing of my mind and my thought patterns. Changing this behavior was not easy, but it was worth every prayer and every conscious struggle toward the goal of being free from the negative influence of others.

I turned the page to the notes on the second day and read the thought for the day. *"My marriage is over. I will not look back . . . only to the future."*

What day did I realize that? I wondered as I checked the date, July 4, 1989. It hit me like a bolt of lightening! That was the very day that my new husband's wife had died. I was "spellbound." I just sat there and tried to comprehend this divine coincidence.

~

"I tell you the truth, you will weep and mourn while the world rejoices. You will grieve, but your grief will turn to joy."
—John 16:20 NIV—

CAMEO 28

The Accident

Soon after I dreamt about becoming a cameo writer, Bob and I decided on the perfect plan so I could be alone to pray and write the book of my cameo dream.

A meeting had been scheduled for the board of directors of our condo in Florida. As a member, I needed to attend the meeting scheduled for the following Monday. I planned to leave Saturday afternoon and drive down in time for the meeting. That would give me a week to pray and perhaps begin writing before Bob joined me. He planned to fly down. We would spend about ten days there together and then drive home. It seemed perfect.

On Friday, I had my car serviced for the trip. When I got in it to drive home from the service department, the seat had been adjusted for the mechanic who had given it a test drive. I adjusted the seat back to its normal position, and as I did that, a thought entered my mind, "Move the seat further back, at least an inch, in case the air bag gets released." I adjusted the seat further back than usual.

Heavy snow was forecast to reach Tennessee and northern Georgia on Saturday. It would arrive in Kingsport on Saturday afternoon. My plan was to leave around noon on Saturday ahead of the snow. I would be out of the predicted snow area and into southern Georgia before dark and would spend the night there. When I awoke at 7:00 A.M. Saturday morning, the hard rain was already mixed with snow. I hurried to get dressed and load the car, hoping that I could get through the local snow and in front of the snow-storm that was coming earlier than predicted. Roads were already getting slippery, and heavy snow was falling by 9:00 A.M. when I drove out of the driveway. I made it safely to the interstate highway. In about twenty minutes, the snow began turning to rain again. I had outrun the snow, but the rain was coming down in torrents, and snow was not far behind. Traffic was heavy, and there were many eighteen-wheelers on the road.

After driving about an hour in heavy rain, I sensed that I was in danger and that my life was in jeopardy. I wanted to turn around and go back home, but I knew the conditions behind me would make that almost impossible. I had driven in heavy rain hundreds of times in the past. "I will be fine," I thought. Yet never in all my years behind the wheel had I experienced the feeling of uneasiness that was surrounding me that day. I began to pray for safety and asked the Lord to surround me with the power of His love and protection. "Don't let the evil one harm me," I asked. I thought of the Scripture that says, *"He will command His angels concerning you to guard you in all your ways"* (Ps. 91:11). I was extremely aware of the mission I was on: writing a book about the Holy Spirit. The stacks of reference books and Bible translations filled the backseat. I knew that I was on a mission trip for the Lord and that the evil one was going to try to stop me. I prayed continuously.

On the interstate just outside the city limits of the town where my former husband and his wife live, my car hydroplaned. It lifted up as if it were on water skis at about fifty-five miles an hour. The left front of the car crashed into the four-foot-high concrete abutment on my left. I heard the crash. The next thing I knew, I was looking down at my half inflated airbag. "It didn't work," I thought. Then I looked up and saw that my car was spinning across the highway and headlights from cars were coming toward me. There was a stunning jolt! With relief I thought my car had stopped. I looked up again only to see it heading, at a terrific speed, straight for a guardrail and embankment. I had no protection now from my airbag, which was totally deflated. Instinctively, I pushed the brake to the floor and turned the steering wheel as far to the left as I could. I watched as my car sped toward the guardrail. There was another crash, a rapid spin, and a sudden stop. The right front of my car had hit the guardrail, spun around on the narrow shoulder, and was now facing on-coming traffic that fed onto the interstate.

I was stunned for a moment. When my mind cleared, I saw that smoke was coming into the car. I pulled on the hand break, released my seat belt, and got out of the car. I suddenly became extremely alert. Realizing that the engine was still running, I got back into the car, turned off the engine, turned on the emergency flashers, and retrieved my cell phone which was on the passenger-side floor. As I reached for it, I saw, in the mirror, that my face was bleeding. I got back out of the car and dialed 911. A young man in a red truck pulled in behind my car. He had been involved in the accident too but was not hurt. He helped me give the rescue people our location. "Yes," I told the voice on 911, "I think I do need an ambulance."

The rain had slowed to a drizzle, and it did not seem cold. I realized that I might go into shock at any moment. I dialed my former husband's home phone. The number, although I seldom had occasion to call it, was crystal clear in my mind. He and his wife were the only people in that town that knew me and might be able to help if I became unconscious. They were home and would come right away.

As I stood there by the car, the young man with the red truck encouraged me to get back into my car to stay warm. Just after an ambulance rushed me to the hospital, my former husband and his wife arrived at the scene of the accident. They were instrumental in getting my car towed, and they also retrieved my glasses and brought them to the emergency room. They stayed with me until I was released later that afternoon. At their invitation, I went home with them until Bob, who was snowed in, could make the trip to get me the following Monday.

The accident that I had just survived with minor injuries could have easily been a fatal one. Resting on a bed in the home of my former husband and his wife, I praised God and thanked Him for sending His angels to protect me during the accident. Then I asked Him, "Dear Lord Jesus, why am I here?" Knowing there must be a reason, I had to smile.

Caroline and the Wind

A few years ago my granddaughter, Caroline, who was five years old at the time, and I were in the car running errands. She was very chatty, and we had some very interesting conversations. On our way home, Caroline suddenly responded to something I said by putting her hands on her hips, shaking her head, and with great emotion puckered her lips and said, "Grandmother, I don't even know if there *is* a God! You can't see Him, and I don't know He is there!"

Before I had time to think how to answer, the Holy Spirit reached out to help me. Just as Jesus taught us in Luke 12:12, *"For the Holy Spirit will teach you in that very hour what you ought to say"* (NKJV). I looked up, and we were passing a post office. I heard myself saying, "Caroline do you see that American flag?" "Yes," she said. Then I asked her, "Do you see it blowing in the wind?" "Yes," she said again. "Do you see the wind?" I asked. "No," she answered. "Then how do you know there is wind?" She answered, "Because I can see it moving the flag!" "Well," I said, "like

"Do you see the wind blowing the flag?"

you don't see the wind, but you see it moving the flag . . . so it is with God. The Bible tells us 'God is love.' When a person is filled with love (that is God) you see God (love) through a person's actions. The Bible calls these actions fruit. What you see is a person filled with love, joy, peace, patience, kindness, goodness, faithfulness, gentleness, and self-control: the fruit of the Spirit."

". . . God has poured out His love into our hearts by the Holy Spirit, whom He has given us"
—Romans 5:5 NIV—

CAMEO 30

Insight to Forgive

Each year, the highlight of my life is attending the National Conference on the Holy Spirit held by *Aldersgate Renewal Ministries* (ARM), the same organization mentioned earlier as UMRSF. The name Aldersgate comes from the name of the street in London where John Wesley felt his heart "suddenly and strangely warmed."

The National Conference on the Holy Spirit is held in a different part of the country each year. Many workshops and seminars are offered on enriching life and ministry. There are praise and worship services, music, and liturgical dancers. Hundreds of people from various denominations attend the three-day conference where many are filled with the Holy Spirit and experience physical and emotional healing. Words cannot express these joyful and wonderful conferences where God is present among us reaching individuals.

A couple of years ago, I attended a workshop at an Aldersgate conference entitled "Learning to do what Jesus did." In Luke 4:18–19 Jesus said: *"The Spirit of the Lord is upon me, because he hath anointed me to preach the gospel to the poor; he hath sent me to heal the brokenhearted, to preach deliverance to the captives, and recovering of sight to the blind, to set at liberty them that are bruised, to preach the acceptable year of the Lord."* In this workshop, we learned the basic principles for healing the sick as Jesus did.

One part of the course taught the importance of accepting forgiveness for things we have said or done in the past. Guilt keeps people from the freedom necessary to live a full and abundant life. We said a group prayer confessing our sins and accepting the forgiveness offered to us through Jesus' death on the cross. Jesus was perfect, and when He died, it was in our place and for the sins we have committed either known or unknown. I prayed with the group.

Next, we prayed silently for ten minutes asking the Lord to show us anyone that we needed to forgive. Then we silently said the name of each person and told him or her in our imaginations that we wanted to forgive him or her. "Even if you can't forgive them right now," our leader said, "go through the motions and say their name and tell them you forgive them. Just by recalling a situation and saying a name, you can begin to forgive. Begin now, and keep doing it until you have forgiven them," he said.

At this point, I felt pretty good because I had done a great deal of forgiving over my lifetime. I had realized years before that I did not want to be bitter or angry. I had no joy with anger and bitterness inside. Yet, I knew that I was not as free as I wanted to be.

About five minutes into the silent prayer, I was asking the Lord to show me anyone that I needed to forgive. I had drawn a blank. Every situation or person that I felt I needed to forgive, I had forgiven. It was then that our leader, who was silently praying too, said, "I am getting the name Ruth. Does Ruth mean anything to anyone?" Well yes, I thought, I had an Aunt Ruth. I began praying then and asking the Lord to show me if I needed to forgive Aunt Ruth for anything. During that prayer, I began recalling a part of my childhood that was all but forgotten.

Aunt Ruth and Uncle Macon lived with my grandmother and taught in a country school about three miles from home. After a few years, Uncle Macon was elected county school superintendent. His office was in Victoria, about twenty miles away. Aunt Ruth continued teaching the seventh grade, which was a difficult grade to teach because of the age of the children. When I visited Granny at Plantersville, Aunt Ruth and Uncle Macon were always there. I loved Aunt Ruth. Sometimes she and I would have a picnic, and for adventure, would walk to interesting places to eat our sandwiches. Sometimes she brought each of us a cucumber fresh from the garden.

Then I remembered the loose tooth, my first. I had never had a loose tooth before, and I was scared. Aunt Ruth offered to "pull it out" for me. I didn't like that idea at all. "I tell you what let's do," she said, " I will tie a string around it and then tie the string to the doorknob." "You won't pull it out?" I fearfully asked. "No," she said. Trusting her, I let her put the string around my tooth, and then I watched her tie the string around the doorknob. No sooner had she tied the string to the doorknob than she slammed the door shut, yanking my tooth out. I was unhurt, but was terrified and in tears. "You told me you wouldn't pull my tooth," I cried. "I didn't pull the tooth," she said, "the door did."

Next, I remembered another disappointment that came from Aunt Ruth. Granny's home was only about a three-hour drive to Richmond, Virginia, where my family enjoyed shopping. I loved to go with them and ride the escalators. Escalators were something new and were only in large, fabulous department stores like Thalheimers and Miller & Rhodes. Those were Aunt Ruth and Aunt Martha's favorite places to shop. I remember that Auntie and Unkie were at Plantersville with me, and the plan was to get up early in the morning and drive to Richmond to shop. I was very excited about the trip. "Please get me up when you get up," I begged Aunt Ruth who had just told me that they would let me sleep while they got dressed. I kept begging to be awakened when my two aunts got up. She kept insisting that I should sleep as late as possible and that it would not take me long to dress. I needed the sleep. I really wanted to get up with them and kept begging until Aunt Ruth finally agreed to call me when they got up.

To my surprise, they were up and dressed when Auntie got me up that next morning. I went to Aunt Ruth saying, "You promised to get me up when you got up." "No," she said, "I promised to call you. I stood out in the hall and quietly called your name and you didn't wake up." How disappointed I was that morning! I don't know why I wanted to be up early with them. I think that I just wanted to be in on all of the excitement of getting ready. We had a great time together in Richmond that day.

Several days after we had enjoyed a wonderful Sunday afternoon of ice cream at the church, I asked Aunt Ruth if she would make some ice cream for us. She consented to make it. She used an old-fashioned ice cream maker where the custard is placed into a metal container inside the wooden barrel-shaped freezer. Rock salt, the large granule kind, and ice were added around the metal container. Next, the crank had to be turned until the ice cream was frozen. As the ice cream froze, the salt melted the ice and became salty brine. I think Aunt Ruth thought that I would turn the crank. I did turn it for a while, but as the ice cream began to freeze, it became more difficult to continue. I soon got tired and asked her if she would turn the crank for a little while. I left her and ran off to play.

When I finally decided to check on Aunt Ruth and the progress of the ice cream, I ran toward the house and stumped my big toe on a rock. It was scraped pretty badly and was bleeding. I ran to Aunt Ruth who was still turning the crank and was unhappy that I had deserted her for so long. She looked at the toe and told me to put it in the melting salty brine. "Will that help it?" I asked her cautiously. She assured me that it would. So, trusting her, I stuck my injured toe into the salt. Out it came with me screaming and crying. The pain was terrible. Aunt Ruth laughed and said that the salt would help it get well. I can still remember the pain caused by that salt in my wound. I never forgave Aunt Ruth but forgot about the incident and was unaware that I needed to forgive her. I hope she forgave me for staying away until the ice cream was frozen.

Over the years, I only remember my daddy visiting me in the country at Granny's on one occasion. He came unexpectedly one morning while Aunt Ruth was punishing me for something I had playfully said the night before. I don't remember the word, and I don't think I knew what it meant, but what I do remember is that I said something that I thought was funny. Granny laughed, and so did I. I think that Aunt Ruth laughed too. So I said it again. Aunt Ruth told me not to say it again, but I did. This time she said that I would have to sit in a corner for thirty minutes if I said it again. I thought she was joking, so I said it again. She added thirty minutes each time I said it and all of the time I thought she was joking. Finally, after I continued to say whatever it was, Granny said, "Donna, you had better not say that again; she really means you will have to sit in a corner for thirty minutes each time you say it." I stopped immediately, but it was too late to avoid about six hours of punishment.

The next day after breakfast I had to go sit on the sofa in the corner of the living room. I could not leave the sofa for six hours. I had been there for almost two hours when I looked out of the window and saw my daddy coming up the walk to the front porch. "Daddy's here, Daddy's here," I remember calling out to Granny and Aunt Ruth who were somewhere else in the house. My Daddy surprised all of us with a visit to see me. Even though this was such a special time for me, as I had not seen him for a long time, Aunt Ruth didn't let me off of the sofa even to give him a hug. I stood on the sofa, though, and he came and hugged me there, never guessing that I was being punished. He sat with me and we talked a while before he asked me to come with him to take a walk. I was mortified for him to know that I was being punished for something I had said. I had to tell him, though, and let him know that I couldn't leave the sofa. He was kind. He said, "Well then, I will just stay here with you." He sat with me until almost time for him to leave. He was only there for a few hours. As he left, Aunt Ruth told me my time was up, and I could leave the couch. It was too late to walk with Daddy. I never had the opportunity to be with him at Granny's again. As I write this almost sixty years later, tears come to my eyes, as I remember the humiliation and disappointment I suffered that day along with the loss of a wonderful opportunity to spend some time with Daddy.

I am still working on forgiving Aunt Ruth, and others, as the Lord helps me recall long-forgotten incidences in my childhood. I repressed much of my childhood because it was filled with emotional pain. Gradually, others that I need to forgive are revealed to me. Aunt Ruth loved me, even though she had a way of hurting me without understanding what she was doing. Years later, it was Aunt Ruth and Uncle Macon that paid my way through college. Aunt Ruth was wonderful to write to me at least once a week while I was away from home that first year.

~

"For if you forgive other people their failures, your Heavenly Father will also forgive you. But if you will not forgive other people, neither will your Father forgive you your failures."
—Matthew 6:14–15 PHILLIPS—

CAMEO 31

Imaging Prayer

𝒯he awesome opportunity to join in praise, worship, and prayer each week with the staff of Aldersgate Renewal Ministries is another highlight in my life. As a volunteer staff member, I work beside and with a wonderful team of individuals that God has brought together for Him to minister to the world.

During one of these weekly praise and worship times, the most amazing thing happened. We praised and worshipped God for about twenty minutes, and then each of us began praying silently. I was led to pray for my son, the whistler turned pilot. I began praying an imaging prayer that God's light would come into my son's condo and drive out any darkness there. I had begun by imaging God's light coming in the front door, into the half bath by the door, into the kitchen, living room, sunporch, up the stairs, and into the guest bedroom and bath, down the hall, and into my son's bedroom. Deep in prayer, I was imaging this light of Jesus overcoming and pushing out all darkness from every nook, corner, and cranny. As I prayed, one of the staff members stood up and gave this prophecy, "And God said, let there be light. And there was light and the light could not be overcome by darkness." She sat back down. I was stunned and said nothing.

In a few minutes, she stood back up and said, "This is not the kind of prophecy that I am usually given. I feel it is for someone in this room or for someone that is known by someone in this room." "It's for me," I said. "I was sitting here praying and imaging God's light overcoming all darkness in my son's condo and ultimately in his life."

After that, everyone gathered around me, laid hands on me, and prayed for my son. What a joyous occasion! I could hardly wait to tell him what had happened during praise and worship that day.

～

"Follow the way of love and eagerly desire spiritual gifts, especially the gift of prophecy. But everyone who prophesies speaks to men for their strengthening, encouragement and comfort."
—1 Corinthians 14:1, 3 NIV—

CAMEO 32

Insight through Prayer

During a pleasant conversation one evening, as we were getting ready for bed, Bob and I talked about some of the fun things that we had done during the day. During the conversation, I said something that triggered a violent reaction in Bob. Neither of us can now remember what it was, but it made him furious, and his behavior was totally inappropriate. Suddenly his voice became loud and rude. He beat on the bed with his fists and called me a bitch. This was not the first time that I had seen this otherwise gentle man show a quick temper.

Silently, and without his knowing it, I entered that "secret room" and began to pray. I don't remember the exact prayer, but it went something like this: "Father in heaven, please help Bob to overcome whatever causes him to be so angry. Open his mind to the truth, and help him to see the real cause of his anger and to deal with it and be healed! Help me to respond to him in a helpful way to build him up and not cause hurt. Let me see him through Your eyes and respond to him with Your love. Don't let me say or do anything that You do not direct."

We went to bed, both of us in a semi-state of shock, he for having reacted like he did, and I for not understanding why.

The next morning was sunny and beautiful. After breakfast we went for a long walk on the beach and talked about many things, with neither of us mentioning the night before. Later in the morning, near lunchtime, we stopped on the beach to rest from our walk and eat a bite together. While we were waiting for our food, Bob said, "Do you know what I think?"

"No, tell me," I said.

"I think there is a little demon of anger that has haunted the Maddox family for several generations! My grandfather used to have a quick temper. My daddy had a quick temper too! My grandmother, Elizabeth Maddox, suffered because of it; my mother, Grace Maddox, suffered because of it; my first wife, Marjorie Maddox, suffered because of it; and now, Donna Maddox suffers because of it!"

It was exciting for me to see how quickly God had begun answering my prayer. He certainly had opened Bob's mind to the truth. Now he was free, and healing could begin.

⌒

"Then you will know the truth and the truth will set you free."
—John 8:32—

CAMEO 33

Something about That Name

£ate one evening, Bob had settled in bed reading the Bible while I was working at the computer. When I finally turned off the computer and knelt by the bed to say my prayers, Bob turned off his reading light. As I climbed into bed we said our "goodnights" and settled down to sleep. Almost asleep, I suddenly felt emotional and raised up in the bed and said, "Bob?"

Bob answered, "Yes, what is it?"

"I just wanted to say your name," I told him.

Bob then turned toward me and said, "You know, I was saying to myself the name of Jesus! I was saying the words of the song, 'Jesus, Jesus, Jesus, there's just something about that name.' I was calling His name and thinking how beautiful it is."

I believe the Holy Spirit in me responded to Bob's praise and caused me to say, "Bob, I just wanted to say *your* name!"

CAMEO 34

Understanding the Prophecy

God's plan for the writing of this book began being revealed to me in the late 1960s or early 1970s when my family began attending Saturday evening Bible teaching at the home of friends. They paid expenses for a wonderful Bible teacher to come from North Carolina to teach in Tennessee every other week. It was interesting how we learned about this opportunity.

My first husband and I attended our Sunday school class in a Methodist church. One Sunday our teacher, Jim, brought Blair Reid to teach the class. He taught directly from the Bible. I was spellbound! The Bible came alive right in our class! After I got home, I called Betty, the wife of our teacher, and asked, "Who is that man who taught our class?" She told me a little about Blair and invited us to join their home group.

The meetings were wonderful. He held us captivated for hours. We would completely forget the time, and often it would be ten or eleven o'clock at night when he prayed the last prayer. Then Betty would invite us into the kitchen for special treats. Bread pudding was Blair's favorite dessert, so we often had that. Soon, each of us brought food and snacks to share. What wonderful discussions and camaraderie we shared.

One Saturday, Blair brought with him a man from Canada named Brother George. Brother George had been teaching in North Carolina when Blair met him. He was one of twelve men in a Canadian church who had a special vision and anointing from God. They were part of a church called "The Church of the New Testament." On Saturday nights, we enjoyed hearing Brother George speak. It was almost like being in one of those small secret groups that is mentioned in the New Testament. As we left the meeting one Saturday night, Betty told us they would have church there in the morning and we were welcome to attend.

Sunday morning I awoke early, eager to go to the church service. My husband decided not to go but encouraged me to attend if I wanted to. He took care of our son. When I arrived at their home, Betty had a little lace doily-like head covering for me to wear during church. For a woman to wear a head covering in church was biblical, and the church in Canada honored that.

There were about eight other people there besides me. Brother George asked me, "Did you come to receive the Holy Spirit?"

"I don't know," I answered.

He told me then that they were having a baptism service, and I was welcome to receive the Holy Spirit.

"Yes, I want to," I said. I was excited because I didn't even know there was a baptism in the Holy Spirit. I had never learned in church about the baptism. I believe the Lord had gotten me up that Sunday morning to empower me for ministry.

As Brother George baptized me, he laid hands on me, and I began to speak in tongues. He prayed a beautiful prayer and suddenly spoke a prophecy for me from God. Betty wrote the prophecy down on a piece of paper and gave it to me as I left.

"This is pretty close to what Brother George said," she told me. "I couldn't remember his exact words."

> My child, I have been with you in all the events of your life and in the things you have suffered. I have known the sufferings you have been through when others did not know. I have a great work for you to do. . . . You will help to bear the sufferings of others and intercede on their behalf. Your hands will minister to their needs.

The whole morning was filled with so much excitement and newness that I would not have remembered the words of the prophecy at all if Betty had not written them down for me. One thing, though, that Brother George said to me that morning stayed in my mind. "There is something about the hands. I am not sure what it is, but there is something about the hands that is involved," he said.

Because I was a nurse, I always thought that I was supposed to do something related to nursing by ministering to people with my hands. I really never practiced bedside nursing. I did become a disaster nurse and served through American Red Cross, both as a volunteer and supervisor on the national disaster reserve team. Although I served on several large disaster assignments, I never felt that "my hands were ministering to their needs" in the way the prophecy meant. Certainly, nothing I accomplished could be classified as "a great work" as mentioned in the prophecy.

Before we left that Sunday, Brother George explained to us that soon after a person is baptized in the Holy Spirit, Satan attacks to try to discourage us and plant doubts in our minds. "Just be aware of this," he said.

That awareness helped me through the inevitable attack. In fact, the attack even strengthened my faith because I recognized it and did not allow it to shake the wonderful gift I had received. That is another story. When I got home, I placed the little handwritten note that Betty had given me in my jewelry box.

Although the other families in the small group soon left the Methodist church to join the Church of the New Testament, I never did. I would have left in a heartbeat, but I felt like the Lord said to me, "Learn and worship Me with the group but stay in the Methodist church. Someday I have a work for you to do there."

Many wonderful years were spent worshipping with that close group of friends and believers. What joyous times we had together. There was praise and worship and prophecies both spoken and sung. A spirit of community surrounded us. We were a family. When Betty and Jim went to England, Betty brought back gifts for each of us. My gift was a lovely cameo pin.

Over thirty years have passed, and it is now February 2000. Nearly every morning, I get up between 5:30 and 6:00 A.M. to pray and to write as the Spirit leads me. I am certain that the Lord wants me to write this book of love cameos. Each morning He confirms this to me in different ways again and again, and I am blessed and get more excited with each revelation.

Recently, I had been looking for the little piece of paper with the prophecy Betty had written down for me more than thirty years ago. Having moved several times, it had been misplaced. I hoped I had not lost it forever. I have read and reread the prophecy over the years to see if I was doing anything related to it, but I never seemed to be. Another thing I had not seen for almost thirty years was the little pin that Betty had bought for me in England. It, too, was misplaced.

One afternoon, without thought, I went directly to the box where the prophecy lay. I lifted the top, not even knowing what I was looking for. The paper was now fragile and yellowed. I was thrilled to find it and was greatly relieved that it was not lost. "Thank you, Lord," I said as I placed it in one of the little sections of my jewelry drawer where it would be protected and easy to find.

That evening, I was looking for a particular piece of jewelry that I wanted to wear and was digging around in one of my jewelry boxes trying to find it. I didn't find it, but there, in the bottom of the box, was the pin that Betty had given me! I was very pleased to find it. I opened my jewelry drawer and put it in there for safekeeping.

Handwritten prophecy.

The next morning, I went to my jewelry drawer to get my rings. The paper with the prophecy was in the middle of the drawer, and on top of it was the cameo pin that I had hurriedly put in the drawer the day before. I had not realized where in the drawer I had put either of them.

Suddenly, it hit me like a bolt of lightning that Betty had given me a cameo! The cameo was now lying on the prophecy she had written down for me thirty years ago. I carefully unfolded the paper and began to read. This time when I read the prophecy, I knew that it was being fulfilled. The last line in particular now took on special meaning. I had never before been able to understand how it fit into my life. "Your hands will minister to their needs." My excitement mounted as I thought of my hands typing into the computer the inspirations given me by the Holy Spirit to share with others. The little cameo pin that Betty had given to me also took on special meaning as I held it in one hand and the prophecy in the other. I will cherish this confirmation always!

Because we no longer lived in the same city, Betty, Jim and I had not talked with each other for several years. I felt compelled to call them and share this wonderful revelation with them. It was great chatting with the two of them on the phone. I told them that I was writing love cameos that lifted up Jesus and the Holy Spirit in my life. Then I shared my exciting news about the appearance together of the cameo pin, a gift from Betty, and the paper with the prophecy written in Betty's handwriting given to me more than thirty years ago.

Here is the next thriller! Jim told me, "One of the men from Canada is coming today, and we will be meeting with him tonight." He also said that three other people, friends from the early days, would be meeting with him that night. I was pleased beyond measure that my testimony could be shared with that special little group that played an important role in the development of my walk in the Spirit. They remain a part of my spiritual family.

Because of God's timing, and their meeting together, I believe it was His desire for them to know about the prophecy and be encouraged.

What a blessing to know that He is the Way, the Truth, and the Light! What a joy to know that His Holy Spirit lives in me, guiding, teaching, and revealing His truth in special and marvelous revelations as I live and breathe and have my being in Him.

~

"God who made the world and everything in it, since He is Lord of heaven and earth, does not dwell in temples made with hands. . . .
For in Him we live and move and have our being. . . ."
—Acts 17:24, 28 NKJV—

Rock of Ages.

～

"My prayer is not for them (His disciples) alone. I pray also for those who will believe in me through their message, that all of them may be one, Father, just as you are in me and I am in you. May they also be in us so that the world may believe that you sent me. I have given them the glory that you gave me, that they may be one as we are one: I in them and you in me. . . ." (John 17:20–23)

～

"God's word—that sacred mystery
which up to now has been hidden in every age
and every generation, but which is now as clear as daylight to
those who love God. They are those to whom
God has planned to give a vision of the wonder and splendor
of His secret plan for the nations. And the secret is simply this:
Christ in you! Yes, Christ in you bringing with Him
the hope of all the glorious things to come!"
—Col. 1:26–27 PHILLIPS—

About the Cameos

 he Lord wants a carved cameo for the cover of the book," I told Stephen Sawyer, "and He has sent me to you."

Months later, Steve had completed the cameo. He had carved Jesus praying, and had named the cameo "Rock of Ages." An angel wing could be imagined as well as a shadow nail print on the oversized hands. It was beautiful, but different from what I had expected. After several days in prayer I understood. At the end of the book was to be the picture of Jesus in prayer for you and me. "Yes!" I thought. "That prayer is what my whole book is about! My book's dedication is to Jesus, the Rock."

I commissioned Steve to carve a second cameo for the book cover and to possibly be made into jewelry. We both drew blanks as to what God wanted on that cameo. One Saturday morning I awakened with a great desire to go to the mall to walk. An antique show was in progress. As I walked by one booth, I noticed a large collection of cameos. My heart raced as I realized the Lord had something for me to see. I was quickly drawn to two cameos. One looked like the cameos of my dream, with its frame and white image carved from a green gem. The other gave me the idea for the "Christ in Me" cameo.

Green represents life. The frame offers a hint of a cross as eyes follow the three projections on each side of the frame. The projections are reminders of the "Father, Son, and Holy Spirit."

My dream had three cameos. In prayer, I asked the Lord about the third cameo. In His quiet voice, He spoke to me, "The book is the third cameo. It has the same single message as the two carved cameos. The message is for my people."

About the Author

$\mathcal{D}$onna Maddox was born in Petersburg, Virginia, and grew up in Radford, where she lived with her aunt and uncle. She holds degrees from Radford University as an honor graduate with a major in psychology, Vanderbilt University with a major in nursing, and Certification in Marketing from the American Society for Hospital Marketing and Public Relations (TSHMPR).

The mother of one son, Maddox spent her early years at home and as a volunteer in the community. Later, she joined the faculty of East Tennessee State University, where she taught nursing for several years. She went on to work as a nurse recruiter and then public relations director for a Kingsport hospital. She is founder and president of Marketing & Business Consultants, Inc., which offers physician and health-care marketing.

Maddox has been listed in Outstanding Young Women of America, Who's Who in Nursing, and was named 1986 Woman of the Year by the Altrusa Club of Kingsport.

The first woman invited to join the Kingsport Rotary Club, Maddox is a member of the Vanderbilt University School of Nursing adjunct faculty as a consultant in marketing and career planning. She is a member of Sigma Theta Tau International Honor Society for Nursing, a life member of International Association of Business Communicators, and a sustaining member of Junior League of Nashville. She serves on the council for Aldersgate Renewal Ministries, a Methodist organization, and on several boards of directors.

She and husband, Bob, enjoy homes in Nashville, Tennessee, and on Longboat Key, Florida.